GOOD MORNING, MORNING GLORY

Good Morning, Morning Glory

When the flower of your life dies

GEORGE D. MANJOUNES

CYPRESS HOUSE PRESS
FORT BRAGG, CALIFORNIA

GOOD MORNING, MORNING GLORY

Copyright © 1996 George D. Manjounes

For information, contact the publisher:

Cypress House Press
155 Cypress Street
Fort Bragg CA 95437
1-800-773-7782

Publisher's Cataloging-in-Publication
Manjounes, George D.
  Good morning, morning glory: when the flower of your life dies
/ George D. Manjounes
  p. cm.
  LCCN: 96-84282
  ISBN: 1-879384-30-2

1. Death — Fiction.   2. Grief — Fiction.   I. Title.
PS3563.A656G664 1996   813'54
                                QB196-20321

Cover design by Mark Gatter

First Edition

1 3 5 7 9 10 8 6 4 2

Manufactured in the U.S.A.

Dedication

In loving memory of Despina Ann Nicolaides

For

Despina Ann (D'Ann) Valsecchi

John G. Manjounes

Alexandra Despina Valsecchi

Paulina Katherina Valsecchi

Fulvio Valsecchi

Never Forget

Sé Ágapô Poly Poly

Acknowledgments

I AM DEEPLY GRATEFUL to many people for their kindness.

A very special thank you to Mary Fiske of New Pensmith who typed the first draft of scribbled words;

Marcy Heidish, novelist, of Approach and Avoidance Editorial, for her advice, inspiring words and blessings;

Alison Whyte, editor of the Editorial Department Inc. for her in-depth analysis of the first draft and inspiring words;

Keira Geffken Sowards for her untiring weekend typing, editing and belief that *Good Morning, Morning Glory* has a very special message;

John Fremont, senior editor at Cypress House for his insight and vision;

Robert and Monica Cugno for their unfailing belief in my writing of *Good Morning, Morning Glory*;

Arthur and Chris Spilios of Loyal/Crown Services for their kindness and production of *Good Morning, Morning Glory* Gourmet Coffee;

And to the very special people who touched upon my life:

Laurie Cortwright
Emily Steward
Karen Tramuta

Raquel Balcolm, a young and caring friend who was present when I felt the absence;

François Paul Lopez Gregorio and lovely Loretta of Cabo San Lucas, BSC Mexico;

And from California: Stacy, Lori, Amy, Liddy, Diane and Mike. Thanks for the memories (Cabo '94);

Georgie! (Pops);

To the beautiful lady who captivated me with her angelic innocence for a moment in time, on an elevator in the Kowloon Shangri-La, Hong Kong, fourth week of May, 1994;

To Cyd Miller, Debra Wood, and Emma Bahta, who always wanted me to read to them;

And to all the women in the world — I embrace you with my words and thoughts — *Sé Ágapô Poly Poly.*

GOOD
MORNING,
MORNING GLORY

CHAPTER 1

MORNING AFTER MOTHER'S DAY

"KAW-KAW, KAW-KAW." A raven's call awakened me. My eyes opened to a sun-filled courtyard. In the still heat, I searched for movement in the branches, bushes and plants, then I lay in bed complaining to myself and to Savannah Lady that we were in for a scorcher of a day. I could not feel or identify the slight hint of a breeze.

Having lived on Hilton Head Island for five years, I could tell by looking out into my bedroom yard that the stillness of the plants and bushes, radiantly gleaming on a sunlit morning, without doubt signaled another hot summer day.

As my eyes searched the yard again, all the beauty in the world seemed contained in the atrium-like courtyard.

The bedroom had a glass partition and the sliding glass door was always open. I loved to sit up in bed and stare through the screen into the courtyard and tell myself that this was it! This was what life was all about: a tranquillity I could identify with. The tall pine, thick and round, almost as old as the earth itself, encouraged the bushes and plants at its royal base to flower and blossom secure and protected. Untrimmed and natural, the courtyard distilled the essence of Hilton Head Island. It was a microcosm, the DNA, the living cell and font of the island.

Savannah Lady lifted her head and pressed against my side. I scratched the top of her head and whispered, "Good morning,

Beautiful lady." Then I rolled over to Despina's side.

Her back toward me, she moaned. "Honey," I said, "did you have a nice Mother's Day?"I put my hand around her waist as she lay on her side and again whispered, "Happy Mother's Day, Despina. I love you." My hand moved to her bosom. She placed her hand on mine and held it in place. We spooned gently. I kissed her on the neck, attempting to awake her.

"Please make the coffee and let the dog out; she has to go," she said.

"In a minute," I whispered. "Boy, I wish this were a Sunday rather than a Monday." I pressed myself against her, expressing my desire, but Savannah Lady, our German Shepherd, insinuated all of her ninety pounds between us, loving and kissing Mother, awakening her.

Savannah Lady rarely left Mother's side. Seldom could I embrace Despina without Savannah interfering. She always wanted to express her love to Mother. I had been meaning to take her to a dog motel for a weekend, so I could have an uninterrupted weekend with Despina. The protective German shepherd followed her everywhere: to bed, to the bathroom, everywhere. She barked whenever I held and kissed Mother.

"Savannah," I called, lifting myself from bed and the warmth and comfort of Despina's side. Savannah followed me. We went to the front yard where she would normally parade, squat, and piddle. Her elegant silver-haired rear always made us laugh, for we thought she had the cutest swing any lady could have when she walked. I leaned against the car impatiently waiting for Savannah to find her spot and contribute to the morning's glory.

Hoot, hoot. A pause. Then "Hoot, hoot," again. The beautiful island birds were communicating. The lagoon was motionless and the century-old trees drooping with Spanish Moss seemed to be reaching up to the heavens. Taking a dog out early in the morning when you're only half-awake can be a tolerable, even enriching experience if you take your coffee with you.

On Mother's Day we'd had dinner at Fulvio's home. I'd stuffed myself with his classic cuisine and, as a result, I now felt lethargic. The stillness of the day prevailed over the melodic call of the birds. The distant deep green fairway highlighted two white cranes on the bank of the lagoon.

The transition of moving to Hilton Head Island from busy city life had taken us five years, but leaning on Despina's car, half naked, half asleep, moved by the ancient beauty around me, I felt I'd always belonged here.

I lifted my head to the trees, their limbs in prayer-like ceremony. Chatter, chatter. Busy birds, all kinds now, were courting or complaining, their calls sounding like psalms chanted and sung by a choir in the service of a divine liturgy — the celebration of morning.

One of the fascinating things about this semitropical island is watching the variety of beautiful birds richly embodied with vivid colors. A blue jay and a little bird with a yellow and red head flew into the yard and landed near the driveway where they began promenading. Two white cranes with long, long necks were watching me. "Man," I said, "this is some magical morning for a guy who's half asleep and watching a dog do her duty."

"You, a bird watcher," Despina would laugh, "I would have never taken you for a bird watcher, George."

"Feed the birds, Al! Feed the fuckin' birds?" I would respond, paraphrasing a friend.

Years ago, our friend Al had married for a second time and moved his new wife from the city to the countryside. At the housewarming cocktail party Jenny, Al's wife, said when asked

3

about how she liked her new home and living in the country, "It shits! And guess what? Al wants me to get up at six o'clock in the morning to feed the fuckin' birds." Despina and I had been laughing about that for years.

Savannah Lady had completed her tour and was hesitantly walking up the driveway. I called her. Her eyes were watching me for a sense of failure to command, so she could run off and play. "Let's go, Savannah," I demanded, and she followed me into the house.

I went to the bedroom. Savannah, realizing my son John was home, dashed to his bedroom. Despina was sitting up. "Hi, Mother," I said. "Coffee will be ready in a minute."

"Please get me some aspirin. They're in my car." She stood and attempted to walk out of the bedroom while I went to find the aspirin.

I was half into her Dodge Colt, fumbling to find the aspirin when I heard a deep piercing scream. "George! Get me the aspirin — George!" I heard another scream as I turned to see my wife, stiff with pain, her arms outstretched against the screen door as if she were being crucified. Pulling myself from the car I ran like a madman while calling out to John. "John! John!" We approached Mother from opposite sides. "What's happening!" we screamed simultaneously.

"John, take Mother's arm."

"Mother's arm won't bend, Dad."

"Crawl under her arm like I have, John!"

Together we drag-walked Mother to the bedroom and sat her on the edge of the bed. Sweat poured down my back, and I trembled with fright.

"What happened, Mother?" John asked.

"I'll be all right," she said. "Just give me my aspirin. I have a

4

terrible headache." Mother sat quietly on the edge of the bed. Her eyes closed, her distinctive oval face contorted in pain. Deep long lines distorted her beauty. A mask of age covered her youthful face.

"I'm calling emergency service!" John shouted in a trembling voice.

A gust of wind rushed by me as my six-foot halfback type son lunged for the phone.

"John, let Mother relax; she has just taken her aspirin. Let's wait a moment; we'll call the emergency service, if we have to."

John sat down beside Mother. He held her hand, then turned toward me. His blue eyes were asking me something, pleading with me. His strong, authoritative face changed into a child's face. Together, mother and child felt the closeness yet, drifted apart, as Mother aged from her pain and John faded into the child — offering the purity of a child's love for the warmth of his mother's embrace.

"Oh, John! Oh, Despina," I cried as I held them both in my arms.

After a moment, when everything seemed to have calmed down, we put Mother to bed and left the bedroom.

"What's wrong with Mother, Dad?"

"I believe she has a serious headache, John."

"Dad, what kind of headache caused her to scream and made her stiff as a board?"

"We'll find out soon. It could be a pinched nerve from sleeping incorrectly. It could be anything I just don't know."

"I'm tired, Dad."

"Me too, John. I feel my blood bubbling through my veins like Alka Seltzer."

"I'm scared, really scared about Mother."

"I know, Son; I am, too. We have to be strong and be there for her — O.K.?"

"All right Dad."

John went to his bedroom. Savannah followed. I went back to my bedroom to find Despina walking toward the bathroom. She lifted her nightgown and sat on the toilet seat. "How do you feel?" I asked.

"Fine. I feel better," she said, going to the wash basin. She rinsed her hands and looked at the wall clock. "It's 7:30. I have to open the store. Doris won't be there this morning."

"Not today. Today, you're going to stay home and rest." With that, I took her by the hand, put her to bed, kissed her tenderly and whispered, "Sé Agapo Poly Poly."

"Sé Agapo Poly Poly," she responded (Greek for "I love you very much").

"I'll get the coffee." I pulled the sheet over her legs, and adjusted the pillow for comfort. She closed her eyes.

I bent over, kissed her again, and left the room to get the coffee. In John's room, both John and Savannah were lying together, their eyes open, concern visible on their faces.

"Mother's resting, John," I said as I walked back to the kitchen to get the coffee.

I poured two half cups of black coffee and carried them back to the bedroom, calling out joyfully, enthusiastically, as if nothing had happened, "Coffee is here." I placed both cups on the night table. "Despina, here's your coffee." As I drew closer, I heard her snore. "Hey, sleepyhead." I patted her on the cheek. Again, a light snore. I paused for a moment. Should I let her sleep? Why is she snoring? She was wide awake a minute ago. "Despina!" There was no response; she was still snoring. "John!" I yelled. "Come here!" I stepped back, looked down at her, then decided to lift her eyelids.

I didn't have to be a medical expert to realize that her stare and wide-open pupils meant she was unconscious. "Despina! Despina!" I called, shaking her in an effort to wake her.

I reached for the phone, fumbled as I dialed 911. John was now in the bedroom. "What's happening, Dad?"

"Mother's unconscious. Lock Savannah in your room." We soon heard distant, screeching sirens.

The phone rang. John answered.

"Who's that?"

"It's the emergency service and the fire department. They are on their way but need specific instructions and location."

As I gave directions to the operator, I looked down at Despina where she lay, unresponsive. Her light brown hair swept backward like rolling waves of a high sea and nestled at the neckline behind her head. Her youthful face wore an angelic smile, her lips were the shape of a pure heart.

A young, earthy, spirited fifty-three year old woman of average looks and height lay before me motionless and radiantly beautiful.

White light hovered over her and all that was imperfect was now perfect.

An unusual energy flowed down from the top of my head. I felt it move down into my legs like a thermometer. I stood there in total shock, looking at a classic lady who would not answer my call the morning after Mother's Day.

My bedroom was soon a parade ground. Men in white were carrying in an array of gadgetry. EKG machines, monitors and other peripheral equipment were set in place, as two men leaned over the bed, over Despina.

Other men were running back and forth through the house. Beepers were beeping, radios were echoing throughout the house. They were communicating with a doctor at the hospital located at the other end of Hilton Head Island.

Amidst it all, Despina lay quietly asleep while oxygen and needles were administered. Blood squirted from her delicate skin, creating streams that looked like hot lava rushing from an erupting volcano. The swift moving, energetic efforts of the valiant men in these emergency groups expressed their total, selfless humanity.

Four men lifted Despina onto a stretcher. Three other men carried the equipment as they rolled her out to the ambulance. "Hey, God! What kind of shit is this! — this magical morning," I called out. Seeing Despina lifted; placed on a cot; rolled out to an ambulance, made me feel as if I had been removed from my environment, placed inside my body and deep within my mind. I stood still, motionless, seeing all, registering nothing. Despina on a cot — men in blue rolling her toward the ambulance. I couldn't do anything, but I silently cried and pleaded to a fading vision of Despina to awake and come down off the stretcher.

"Oh God, John, not our lovely lady! This can't happen to our family," I cried out when I could finally speak.

"Dad, calm down. Nothing has happened. All this will turn out to be a simple check-up and we'll have Mother home this afternoon."

John and I jumped into my car and we followed the ambulance.

I slouched back into the passenger seat as John drove. "John," I said, "I can not and will not believe that anything is seriously wrong with Mother." I looked at him and saw a tear slowly slide down his face. I closed my eyes, leaned back and whispered, "Oh, my God, let nothing be wrong." But the tear moving down the side of John's cheek left no doubt that something was happening to his mother. John was now 27 years, of strong and good character, and rapidly becoming a knowledgeable businessman. This was important to me, but he was too young to lose his mother. I refused to accept the possibility, although John's deep concern gave me a sudden jolt of reality. John broke his silence.

"Dad, Mother will be all right. I love you, Dad." And with that my heart grew heavy. My arms fell by my side, my head fell back and I closed my eyes.

An old familiar feeling came over me. It was a pulling-away feeling, a standing-alone feeling. With a moan, I adjusted myself in the car seat.

"Dad, are you all right?"

"I'm O.K., John."

"Tell me, Dad, what's the matter?"

"No, really, John. I'm O.K., It was just a lonely feeling."

"Tell me, Dad. Talk to me," John pleaded.

"Well, I was thinking about the time that Mother and I were at Grand Central Station. She was an assistant buyer back then for a group of fashion retail stores. As I recall, she had to go to Charlotte for a buyer's convention. We had been married for about a year and this was the first time we were going to be apart from one another. I remember kissing her good-bye and walking away. I looked back, and she was still standing where I had left her. She hesitated to board the train. She wore a yellow dress with some blue flowers on it. I'll never forget that dress. There she stood, silently calling out to me, staring, watching me walk away. A heavy feeling came upon me then. I wanted to stop. I didn't want to walk any further. I looked back again and there stood your mother in her high heels and tight dress, a big round hat on her long light brown hair. There was a glow around her. She was totally Mother and just too lovely to walk away from.

"John, I also felt a strange pulling-away feeling, an empty sort of feeling, as mother was being placed into the ambulance today, the same strange feeling I had years ago."

"You've never had that feeling before this morning?"

"Just once before."

"But you used to leave Mother all the time to go on business trips."

"Yeah, John, but I never had that feeling of leaving one another, like then and now." I closed my eyes, and my head jerked back from a sudden stop at a traffic light. A thought flashed before me, triggered by "like then and now," the beginning and now — the end.

"We're here, Dad," John said as he pulled into the hospital parking space facing a sign that read **EMERGENCY** in big, bold red letters.

The letters frightened me.

We walked through two sets of doors toward a receptionist. I turned to John. "I hate hospitals." There was a strange smell, a hospital smell. I felt antagonistic. "John, I resent being here. We don't belong here. I've never been ill, and no one in the family has ever been hospitalized." Arrogantly, I thought that it was all wrong. We were not a sickly family; and we never would be either.

"Dad! The nurse is talking to you."

My hand went to my forehead, as if to hold on to a thought.

"Jonas," I said. "I'm George Jonas. My wife."

"Oh! Mr. Jonas,. your wife has been taken up for a cat scan. The doctor is on his way and will have a reading in about 20 minutes."

"How is she?"

"Mrs. Jonas is unconscious. The doctor will explain everything after the cat scan," the nurse said, then turned and left. Another lady in a reddish-orange frock with a volunteer patch on her pocket put a cup of black coffee in my hand.

"Thank you."

"We have plenty more," she said as she gave John a cup.

My lips went to the cup. "Just right." I took a big swallow and nodded to John as the coffee warmed my insides.

We had nothing to say, lost in our separate thoughts. John as a son, I as what? Husband? I didn't like that word. Lover? That was inappropriate. Father? That sounded incomplete. What was I? Four years younger than Despina, a little on the heavy side, a workaholic and something of a crazy man. I guess that kept the adventure in our lives. What else? I really couldn't define it. All I knew was that Despina was everything to me, everything in this whole world, and now I was thinking of what I was to her and I was unable to find an answer.

To her many friends she was Dee, and at work she was Miss Dee of the Camellia Room, fashion adviser to women in Vogue, better dress wear. She wore long strands of pearls and would twirl them methodically when women would rush into the Camellia Room calling out hysterically, "Dee, Dee, I need something to wear for Saturday night!"

"John, do you think Mother's frustrations stressed her out?"

"What do you mean, Dad?"

"Well, Mother would get upset with the boutique because they bought merchandise incorrectly."

"Dad, Mother only worked three days a week just to keep herself busy and meet with her girlfriends. The days of Miss Dee the buyer of the Camellia Room, were over when you decided to move here to Hilton Head, six years ago. Mother accepted that. Why are you concerned about her work at the boutique now?"

"Well, Mother's been uptight lately and I thought it might be…"

"Be what?" John interrupted.

"Well, let me finish my thought. It might be that she felt inadequate just being a part-time employee at the boutique."

"That's not it, Dad. Mother's problem is that she's lonely and that's because you started a whole new business again, and you haven't had time for her."

"What the fuck," I sputtered, then fell mute.

John and I continued to watch the hospital activity. Our mutual acknowledgment of the efficient operation was shared telepathically and with eye contact. We moved from the bustling corridor to a comfortable waiting room with many windows, chairs and reading material.

The sun was at its zenith. Heat pierced the windows; bright light scoured the corners of the room for remnants of darkness. The pure light attracted me toward a window into which rays of pure white sun poured. I closed my eyes and experienced a new sensation.

The warmth energized my body, bathed my face. The heat felt great. As soon as I get Despina out of this place, I thought, I'll take her to the white sands of the beach behind the Mariner's Inn. I'll sit there with her and just hold hands. I'll tell her as I so often have over the past 30 years that I love her with my whole being.

She was always asking me to sit beside her on beautiful Hilton Head beach. She could sit for hours, sipping on vodka and grapefruit juice, soaking up the island sun and read. As for me, I would be grilled like a frankfurter within 15 minutes. When the sun became unbearable, I would jump into the cool ocean waters, and look back at Despina reading. She would put her book on her lap and call to me. "George, stay here and read with me. I worry each time you go for a swim," she'd say upon my return.

Please God, let Despina be well, and I'll sacrifice my body to the sun. I'll sit on the beach every day, all day, for the rest of my life. If I could only have now what I could have had then.

My mind was racing. The sun's heat concentrated on my forehead. I tried to break from its bright white light, but I couldn't. Something was holding me firmly in place. I was a child again.

Yia Yia. My grandmother's face with her beautiful long, white hair was coming toward me.

"Georgie, Oh! My Georgie, My *pedi* (child), don't tell your *papou* (grandfather) where we found the birdie."

"O.K., Yia Yia. I won't, Yia Yia."

"Dad!" John called out, "What are you saying?" Taking my arm, he pulled me from the window and from one state of consciousness into another.

"Dad, what was that all about? You scared the hell out of me."

"Oh, nothing," I said, "I was just thinking out loud." What was that all about I wondered, hiding from John the shiver of fear that went through me.

A tall lean man entered the waiting room, dressed in a shabby suit.

"Hello, I am Doctor Spencer."

"Hello," said John. "This is my father."

"I came as soon as I heard about Despina." We shook hands.

"Do you know Despina?"

"Yes, she came to see me about six months ago, and I treated her for high blood pressure."

"High blood pressure?"

"Yes. I prescribed a medication for her."

"What kind of medication?"

"For her blood pressure," he said, as if speaking to a child.

"I was unaware that Despina went to a doctor for any reason. What has happened, Doctor?"

"Mr. Jonas, a blood vessel has broken and one side of your wife's brain is full of blood. I have called Dr. Higgs, and he'll be here in a few minutes. Dr. Higgs is a fine neurologist."

"What does it mean, Doctor?"

"Well, it's like this," Dr. Spencer said. "One side of her brain is full of blood. The blood is putting pressure on her brain. In some cases we can operate, remove the blood, and clip the blood vessel. But, in most cases we lose the patient. Dr. Higgs will know better, but in my opinion, Mr. Jonas, we are going to lose Despina in the next twenty minutes." He raised his hand to prevent me from speaking. "Let's wait for Dr. Higgs' opinion."

"What are you saying?" I cried.

"Dr. Higgs will explain everything." Dr. Spencer left the room.

John and I looked at one another.

"Is this guy for real?" I asked.

"Yeah, Dad, that's exactly what he is — for real — no bullshit. He's telling you like it is. Look, Dad, I don't want to lose my mother." Tears formed in his eyes again. "But as to whether his manner is correct, I don't give a damn. I just want to save Mother."

"John, his mannerism isn't what I meant by 'real'. What I mean is, 'is the thought of losing Mother for real?' And if that's for real, then is the doctor's assessment that Mother will die in the next twenty minutes for real? Tell me John, how are we supposed to handle the next twenty minutes? Tell me, John, Am I to greet death with open arms or am I to kick him in the ass and say 'Go away jughead?' "

"Dad! You're unbelievable! Let's go find Doctor Higgs."

We left the waiting room and encountered the nurse who'd greeted us.

"Nurse, where's Dr. Higgs?"

"Dr. Higgs is waiting for you in the X-ray viewing room, Mr. Jonas. "

John and I rushed to the viewing room. "Dr. Higgs?"

"Yes?" He looked up from his X-rays.

"I am George Jonas and this is my son, John."

"I'm very sorry about Despina," Dr. Higgs said. "Listen very carefully. Despina is unconscious; she's in a coma; we think she's had an aneurysm somewhere on this side of the brain." He pointed to an x-ray. "An aneurysm is a blood vessel that forms a bubble and then bursts. We don't know where in the brain, but one half of the skull is full of blood which is putting pressure on that side of the brain. This is why she's in a coma. If we don't remove the blood and relieve the pressure on the brain, she'll die.

"But, if we operate and drain the blood, there's a chance we may be able to clip the blood vessel and save her life.

"The side of the brain affected is the side that controls her voluntary motor functions, not the side that relates to memory and life sustaining functions.

"If we're successful, with help, she may regain her physical normality."

"Dr. Higgs, please operate, please save her. I don't care about anything else; I'll take care of her."

"I'll start right away, Mr. Jonas." We shook hands and parted.

Unsure of what to do next, John and I waited in the hospital parking lot for D'Ann and Fulvio.

D'Ann, my lovely daughter, was three months pregnant. She didn't show physically, but one could tell from the glow on her twenty-four year old face that she was creating life. Mother and D'Ann were extremely close, good friends. You can be close to your parents, but to also have your parent as a good friend and companion is special indeed.

"John, I am worried about the effect Mother's collapse is going to have on D'Ann's pregnancy."

"What do you mean, Dad?"

"Should anything go wrong, it'll tear D'Ann apart, and I am worried about her unborn baby."

"We'll talk to Dr. Higgs about it, Dad."

"John! We have an appointment this morning with Peterson from the Famous Ice Cream Company."

"God, I forgot all about that!"

"He and Mike Bradshaw are staying at the Mariner's Inn. Call Peterson, tell him what's happened and have them come to our office tomorrow. And John, don't forget to call John McPherson, too. I am going to sit in the car and wait for D'Ann and Fulvio. I can't think straight right now."

John went to make the call. I sat in the car feeling the noon heat crawl over me, remembering.

"George, I am so excited that D'Ann is going to have a baby girl! I can't wait. Just think, you'll be a grandfather. Aren't you excited, George?"

"Despina, I'm not old enough to be a grandfather."

"You mean you can't accept the term 'grandfather' 'cause it places you in a category, reveals your age. Oh you silly little boy. Come here. Let me give Daddy a big hug 'cause Daddy doesn't want to grow up."

A little baby girl, that's it. That will make Despina happy. I've got to get her out of this hospital.

John returned from his phone call.

"Peterson have anything to say?"

"No. He was sorry about Mother and said that a meeting at our office tomorrow will be fine. I called the office. Everything is O.K. there. Our route drivers are out and are very sorry to hear about Mother."

"Well, John, I feel comfortable about not being there. Emily can take care of any problems that come up."

"D'Ann and Fulvio are here, Dad." D'Ann trembled as she got out of the car. Her red brownish hair was swept back like Mother's. In fact she looked like Mother, if perhaps an inch shorter. Her face oval and distinctive, but childlike, was heavy with concern. Her walk was determined as she hurried toward me.

"Dad, I'm afraid for Mother," she said, as she embraced me. "Tell me, what's happening? What did the doctor say?"

"In a moment," I said. I held her tightly and began to cry but not fully, for I wanted to be strong for my family. Whether holding your tears, crying or not crying means that you're being strong for your family, I don't know. I just wasn't going to let go in front of my children.

Fulvio, a tall man originally from Milan, was much older than D'Ann. He reminded me of Raul Julia, the actor.

My sweet and lovely daughter D'Ann was deeply in love with him.

I held on to D'Ann's arm, for I had weakened. I began to relive the last four hours, to the minute, to the second, explaining to D'Ann what had happened. She wanted to know every detail.

John accompanied Fulvio, and the four of us slowly walked back into the hospital.

We were assigned a very comfortable waiting room adjacent to the critical care unit and the emergency surgical room.

D'Ann's eyes were now full of tears; they were not quite running down her cheeks, but pools of water were about to overflow her eyelids. The pools magnified her beautiful green eyes, while reflected light flickered her deep sadness with each movement.

As I looked beyond the tears through the color of her eyes, into the corridors of her mind, I saw the pure agape (love) she had for Mother.

"Oh, Dad, I feel terrible. Mother and I argued the other day. I walked out of the house and went home."

"What was the argument about, D'Ann?"

"Silly things. First it was about the boutique store. How the new manager doesn't know what she's doing 'cause she has no experience and how they buy the wrong kind of merchandise. That's why their sales are down. I tried to tell Mother that it wasn't any of her business, and she got very upset with me."

"D'Ann, Mother's been an advisor to the boutique. She's changed things around and made a great contribution the past few years. Mother won't let go of her life's experience in the fashion world. That's why she works a couple of days a week."

"But, Dad, I thought she came to Hilton Head to get away from it all."

"D'Ann, we're talking about Miss Dee of the Camellia Room," I said, and she smiled with great pride.

Fulvio sat by D'Ann's side and tried to comfort her. His face was pale, astonished; his jaw had fallen, lengthening his face. The weight of this tragic moment clung to Fulvio's jaw; he could not close his jaw.

Despina had become his best friend, and his love for her flowed over him.

It was only yesterday, Mother's Day, that Mama, Fulvio's mother, was honored. She'd been flown in from Milan and had stayed with Fulvio and D'Ann for more than a month.

We got together on Mother's Day to rejoice in mother-to-be D'Ann's luck and happiness, to honor Despina, mother of John and D'Ann, and to honor the mother of all mothers: Mama. She was a small lady of eighty-six with a strong mind and the stamina of an Olympic runner.

"Fulvio, what does Mama eat to keep her so strong and young?"

"Nothing. She drinks wine." His speech still carried vestiges of Lombardy.

"She drinks wine? What kind of wine? Gatorade wine?"

"Red wine, George, red wine."

"Fulvio, I came early this morning to help you move some things around. Now it's late in the day. You and I are exhausted. Mama, though, is in the kitchen cooking. I went to taste her risotto and she whacked me on the hand with a wooden spoon. This morning she cleaned your yard, carried six big logs up your steep stairs, stacked the logs by the fireplace, washed all the clothes in the house, took a three mile hike and, if I am not mistaken, did all this while wearing two sweaters over two heavy dresses with woolen stockings, and she's still cool as a cat. Fulvio, it's 85 degrees outside."

"George, if there were a mountain here, Mama would climb that, too. Have a glass of red wine."

"Hello," said a soft-spoken nurse, disrupting my thoughts as she entered the waiting room.

We all gathered around her. I stared up at her plump baby face and her unusual hat, which signified she had authority over other nurses.

"Mr. Jonas, Dr. Higgs wants you to know that he has removed the blood pressing on Despina's brain."

"That's great!"

"Will that take her out of danger?" asked John.

"Yes, the pressure on the brain has been relieved." The nurse sat down. "Mrs. Jonas will be in surgery for about four more hours. Dr. Higgs is one of the best. He has performed brain surgery often and will do everything possible for Despina." She was kind and genuinely concerned about us.

My eyes moved from her to Fulvio, D'Ann, and John. They all had their eyes fixed on the nurse and listened attentively.

I could tell that her words were being weighed heavily by John. His piercing blue eyes evaluated everything she said. At one corner of his mouth, his lips trembled. He knew full well the danger his mother was in, that she might die.

"Was yesterday the Mother's Day to bid Mother farewell?" I wondered.

If Fulvio had not brought Mama over from Italy, if he had not prepared dinner to celebrate Mother's Day, if there were no Mother's Day, would Mother be conscious, alive with life as before? Would any of this reverse the day's events — reverse the reverse?

My face was unwashed and drained of color. The nurse looked at me compassionately.

"Mr. Jonas, you and John should go home for a few hours. You have been here since early this morning."

John and I agreed to leave, but I felt the gravity of the earth pulling me down, making me heavy. I felt incapable of lifting my legs, but I did.

"My God, John, we forgot to let Savannah Lady out of your bedroom! How are we going to explain this to her? She knows something is wrong. She may be a dog, but her brain is not a dog's brain. She's people, even though she's a German shepherd. She's more human than most humans. Don't you think so, too, John?"

"Yes, Dad. Come on. Let's go home."

"Savannah expresses her sensitivity, love and humanity every day to Mother. Am I right, John?"

"Yes, Dad." He took my arm.

"And love, who knows of love? And not just human love; has anyone ever studied the creative force of love in the mind of a dog and compared it with the creative force of love in the mind of man?"

"No, Dad, I don't think so. You're tired, Dad. Come on, let's go home."

"I'm coming. I'm coming, John." I stopped, blocking the door. "My God... Oh, my God... I haven't thought of God, prayed to God, visualized God or called for God before today. God the forgotten must be called by us today."

"O.K., Dad, let's go home now. I'm tired, too."

I embraced D'Ann tightly, assured her that all would be well with Mother, kissed her tender cheek, felt the purity of her tears that finally overflowed her eyelids, and whispered into her ears, "Sé Agapo Poly Poly. I love you very much."

Sé Agapo Poly Poly was all that remained and was understood by my children of the rich heritage their great-grandparents brought from Greece. Its meaning is deeper than "I love you very much," reaching into the depths of one's soul to express a profound and divine love.

John and I asked Fulvio to care for D'Ann, telling him that we would return shortly.

All the while, the nurse observed how the impact of our emotion and love for Despina filled the room, touching and embracing everyone.

She felt our suffering.

"Hilton Head Island, South Carolina."

"What?"

"I said, 'Hilton Head Island,' John."

"Oh. Look, Dad, I need you now more than ever. Don't go crazy on me."

"What do you mean by that? All I said was 'Hilton Head Island, South Carolina.' "

"I'm not just talking about that."

"What then?"

"You know…" he hesitated. "You were going crazy on me — standing by the window calling out, 'O.K., Yia, Yia. I won't, Yia, Yia.' What the hell was all that about? And then in the waiting room, when we were going to leave, you flipped out."

"John, watch out for the car ahead of you. You're driving too close."

"Don't tell me how to drive the car. O.K., Daddy," he said, as if I was treating him like a child.

"Let's not quibble about stupid situations. Please, John. Let's not quibble, all right?" I squeezed his forearm and said, "I love you, Son."

"I love you, too, Dad."

The traffic eased up. We came to a stop sign.

"John, do we have any scotch at home?"

"No."

"Then let's stop at Herbie's and pick up a bottle. I need a stiff drink."

"Dad, I don't want you to get smashed."

"I won't, but let's face it, we both need a drink. This has been a trying morning." We pulled up to Rock's Party Store.

"John, you go get two black coffees at Rock's and I'll get the scotch from Herbie's."

As soon as I entered the liquor store, Herb called out, "George! What's this I hear about the Mrs.?"

"Yeah! Herb. We rushed her to the hospital this morning. I didn't think you'd be open so early."

"I came in early to get organized. Hope the Mrs. will be all right."

"Hope so too, Herb. Am a-praying," I said, in a native tone. My eyes caught sight of the Jameson's Irish Whiskey. "I'll take a bottle of Jameson's, Herb. Write it up, will you? I left the house without money this morning."

"No problem," Herb said. "Watch out for those hospitals," he added, as he bagged the whiskey.

"Yeah! This is supposed to be a good one, right?"

"Well, it's all right. Better than most. Still got to watch 'em."

"What's your experience with them?"

"No experience with Hilton Head. But the one in Savannah left a sponge in me."

"What?"

"Yeah! They left a sponge in me. That's why I'm bloated."

I chuckled. "Come on now, Herb," I said with concern.

"No shit, George. They left a damn sponge in me."

"Who?"

"Good question. The doctors blamed the hospital, and the hospital blamed the doctors. And I'm suing 'em both."

"Herbie, my good man..." I was puzzled. "I'm going home. I'm going to have myself a drink, sleep, shower and try to wake up to a new day." With that I walked out.

However, my thoughts remained briefly with Herb. I really liked him. I wondered why he was so big and round in the midsection. He really wasn't overweight, sort of stout, but not overweight. Gee, they must have left the sponge in him and it bloated him up. What insanity! Something really went wrong today.

John handed me my coffee. I placed it on the roof of the car so I could open the door. I heard my name called, and I turned to find Abraham walking briskly toward me.

"George, John told me about Despina and am goin' ta' pray for 'er. She's a fine lady, and am going ta' pray for 'er."

"Thank you, Abraham, thank you," I said, with tears in my eyes as we embraced one another.

Black men hanging around the big old oak tree at the far corner of the party store building watched with both curiosity and indifference as the black man embraced a white man.

Abraham worked for me on an as-needed basis for four of the five years I'd lived on the island. He was lean and tall and, above all, a fine man. Black men would gather 'round this big oak tree every morning and wait for white men to pull up with their trucks offering a day's labor for a minimum wage.

Black men hanging 'round waiting for white men seeking help for the day. Still going on — an old Southern tradition.

Somehow I was always bothered by the thought. Yet, whenever I would need help, I'd seek black men hanging 'round the big old oak. That's how I met Abraham, and that's how I'll leave him, for that's the way of the island.

Sea Pines Plantation, majestic and oh! so very beautiful, I thought as we turned onto Duck Pond Road, heading home.

"Look, John, there's Mother's friend, Charlie. He's out of the water. Pull over, John."

Charlie was sunbathing on the far side of the lagoon. "Pull over, John," I said with excitement as I rolled the car window down. "I want to see if I can see what Mother sees in Charlie. Stop here!"

I broke open the Jameson's, raised the bottle to my mouth and swallowed. John did not comment. He allowed me, though I knew he did not like what I was doing. I poured some whiskey into my black coffee, and with that John reached over and took the bottle from me.

"Look at Charlie, John; isn't he big?" I attempted to leave the car, but John grabbed my arm. "Where the hell do you think you're going?"

"I'm going to get a closer look at Charlie."

"Dad, you're not going anywhere. We have enough problems. I don't need my father dragged into a lagoon by a ten foot, thousand pound alligator."

"John, the alligator is asleep. I don't intend to get anywhere near him."

"Close the door, we're going home," he said. "Dad, we have enough problems. Mother may die, Famous Ice Cream is trying to put the screws to us, and you want to play with a killer alligator. What the hell's going on, Dad? What the hell's going on?"

My body stiffened. I sat upright and in a serious, business-like manner I became me again.

"You're right, John. We do have problems, and we are going to handle them together." I paused. "Mother's fascinated with the beauty of that big, old, ugly alligator. Isn't she, John? Wonder how she came to name it Charlie?"

"Yeah! Dad, that is interesting. I know she always stopped to gaze at Charlie. And if Charlie wasn't out, she would be disappointed. There was something special about her appreciation."

"I think I know why Mother is fascinated with Charlie. One time when Mother asked me to stop the car so she could watch Charlie, she commented on how still and quiet he was sitting in the sun."

"She felt Charlie's tranquillity."

"You're right, John. She felt the inner peace, the stillness of silence, the tranquillity of Charlie out of the lagoon bathing in the sun. That's what Mother and Charlie have in common. I wonder if Charlie watched Mother as Mother watched and thought about him."

"Not quite, Dad. Hey let's not get philosophically crazy this morning. The day is crazy enough."

Finally, we arrived home. I got out of the car, leaned on it, and looked around. The light of day gave to all things a brightness of purity, and the purity gave to all things a brightness of color.

The water of the lagoon lay still and mirrored the landscape opposite.

The trees, the homes were a perfect picture ascending from the water real and unreal. The image, in glorious color, embraced the silence. The silence of the moment concerned me, for all I could hear was the silence. Earlier this morning, bird calls awakened me, now there were no singing birds. None of the kaw-kaws, the hoot-hoots, the knocking woodpecker.

The white crane across the fairway was motionless. The sky was high and very blue. The big old trees looked sad. There was no wind; everything was very still, very quiet. Something was happening to me. I felt strange. I pushed open the fiery red door to the house. Savannah Lady jumped frantically all over me. "How the hell did she get out of your bedroom?" John called her and they both headed toward the fairway.

Before he left with Savannah Lady I noticed tears had filled his eyes. I felt torn. Despina was in the hospital; my children, John and D'Ann, were going through a new kind of hell. I felt helpless for I could not make everything right. I felt I was failing them.

Home felt different to me as well.

I went to the kitchen for a glass for the Irish whiskey, then poured and drank two swallows quickly. I wanted to force myself to feel differently. Our living room was full of Ficus trees and plants that were arranged alongside the large windows that walled the house. The view was a golfer's paradise of sculpted fairways and landscaped beauty.

I looked out and saw John walking, throwing a ball for Savannah to chase.

From the initial burning of the whiskey to a warm feeling; from early morning to mid-day on an empty stomach, I now was able to accommodate a new sadness. Yet, strangely, I felt good.

I tilted my head back, closed my eyes, and positioned my face into the noonday sun.

"Oh Despina! Forgive me. What's happening to you should not be."

My face was warming, my eyelids were heavy and Yia Yia's

face appeared, moving toward me, calling out, "Oh Georgie. Oh My Georgie, my child, don't tell your grandfather where we found the birdie."

The child within me said, "I won't tell Papou — Yia Yia, I won't tell."

She kissed me and said, "Sé Agapo Poly Poly."

Still standing, feeling both the warmth of the sun and the Irish whiskey, frightened, I thought about my grandmother serving my grandfather his dinner.

"Eat your chicken, Georgie, my boy. Yia Yia, come and sit down," said Papou.

Yia Yia noticed me staring at my plate. "Eat your dandelions. They are good for you," Yia Yia said.

I was ten years old, visiting my grandparents who loved me dearly.

My grandmother had taken me to the Lynn Beach Walkway that morning, and after an hour or so of splashing barefoot in the tiny waves, we returned home.

We walked through a cemetery. I don't know whether it was a shortcut home, or that grandmother wanted to wish a former friend well, but it was there that my grandmother noticed the dead pigeon lying on a grave. She moved swiftly, calling out, "Oh, the poor dead birdie," as if someone else was going to take it. As she bent down, her long white hair unraveled from the bun behind her head. A summer breeze lifted her hair as she turned toward me and placed the dead bird in her carrying bag. She was beautiful.

"Yia Yia, the pigeon is dead. Poor birdie."

"I know, my Georgie," she said. Then, to the grave: "Forgive me please, may you hold the hand of God forever, you blessed soul beneath my feet. I meant not to trample upon your grave, but we are poor and the bird will serve us well. She made the sign of the cross, took my hand and hurried me out of the cemetery.

"Yia Yia, you're walking too fast for me. Aren't you going to throw the pigeon away?"

"No, Georgie, God sent it to us so that we may have chicken and greens to eat. Don't tell Papou where we found the birdie, promise me, Georgie."

"I promise, Yia Yia."

"Eat your dinner, Georgie," said Papou. "The chicken is good, Yia Yia."

Yia Yia smiled, her head nodded, giving me the approval to eat. I bit into the bird. It *was* good.

The flash of what once was shocked me back to reality. My grandmother's face drifted away echoing, "Don't tell Papou, don't tell Papou where we found the birdie." The stained gray gravestone, Yia Yia praying for forgiveness for walking on someone's grave, and the dead pigeon upon an unkempt grave became fixed in my mind.

The remaining Irish Whiskey in my glass found the path to my larynx in demand of another sensation.

Turning away from the warmth of the sun's rays, I took a shower. I hoped the hot water would wash my thoughts away.

The water felt great. I leaned against the shower wall and turned the hot water faucet to near burning. The water left its warmth on my skin. It was a good feeling, so I stood there, exhausted, burning out. Coming from the shower, I reached for a towel, but none were in place. They were on the floor in a row leading to the bed where there were a dozen more, all blood-stained.

"What's this?" I said aloud. I picked up two of the towels,

held them, then cried into them. "Oh God, let Despina be well." Then I recalled the flow of red blood when the emergency group worked on Despina.

The twenty-minute shower had allowed me to drift from reality, but seeing Despina's blood brought me back. Dressing quickly, I reflected on the morning's experiences.

I remembered bringing in two cups of coffee and placing them on the night table. John and I put mother to bed, adjusting her pillow under her head, kissing her beautiful face, whispering, "Sé Agapo Poly Poly, Despina." Then a fright came over me. I remembered the moment I called her to sit up and have coffee with me and, instead, heard a slight snore. That's when I patted her on the cheek; that's when she would not wake. Just then I thought of what the doctor had said, that her unconsciousness was caused by blood pressing down on one side of her brain. I was going to let her sleep through the morning. Had I done so, I would have killed the mother of my children, my lovely lady.

What prompted me to lift Despina's eyelids, I don't know, but I know now that I was having a struggle with death and his right to claim her.

"John, are you ready? We must rush to the hospital. I know how to save Mother! I know how to save Mother!"

"All right Dad, I'm coming."

"John, give me the keys - I'll drive."

"Oh, no, I'll drive."

On the way back to the hospital, John said, "Dad, what do you mean about knowing how to save Mother?"

"Simple," I said. "Dr. Higgs is operating, the blood has been drained and has released the pressure on the brain. The nurse told us that the immediate danger is over. Now we'll hold her and talk to her. We will reach her and not let her go."

"Right!" said John. He looked me in the eye. His mother was dying, and I was becoming a simpleton, crazy-like.

"John, take your time driving to the hospital. I need to talk with you."

"Dad, I thought you wanted to rush to the hospital."

"I changed my mind."

"Oh! O.K."

"John, this is a difficult time for all of us. You and I have been working together in our business for five years. It's hard for father and son to be together constantly, work together, agree on all things. But, now I not only need you as a son, I want you to go a step beyond and be my friend."

"Dad, I am your friend."

"I know. Hear me out."

"The kind of friend I need right now is someone I can talk to, tell my innermost thoughts to. I am thinking about deep things, deep feelings. Before, I only had Mother; now I only have you. I can only talk to D'Ann to a certain point; she's devastated about Mother. She's got Fulvio and the baby to think of. I feel more comfortable telling you what I am thinking about, because you can handle it."

John reached over, grabbed my hand, pressed it tightly.

Was I placing too serious a burden on John by sharing my innermost thoughts? Did he not have his own thought process to cope with?

We exited Sea Pines Plantation and drove to Palmetto Dunes, Mariner's Inn, Mother's favorite spot. We ordered two glasses of cabernet and sat facing the ocean. The pause from the rush to the hospital afforded us a moment's peace of mind.

"Tell me, Dad, what's on your mind?"

We lifted our glasses of wine and in prayer, toasted Mother

and together we said, "Please, Dear God, keep her well. Let nothing go wrong."

"John, as you know, last weekend I was in Hartsville. The men and I unloaded a trailer load of ice cream. Anyway, that Saturday afternoon, when all was done I went to our office and just plopped myself down on the sofa. I placed my feet up on the sofa arm, elevating my feet, adjusted a pillow under my head, closed my eyes and I died."

"You mean you fell asleep."

"No, I mean I died."

"You mean you fell asleep, Dad. And I wish you would stop using the words dead, die or died, for Christ's sake. Haven't we enough negative stuff to overcome?"

"John, we agreed that we would talk."

"O.K., go ahead."

"John, we are going to have to use the words 'dead', 'die' or 'died' for death is part of life. You can be as positive as you want; in fact, I have always encouraged you to be of positive mind, for that's how I thought I have lived my life. But, now, in relationship to this morning's experiences and your not wanting to refer to the words 'dead', 'die', or 'died', I believe that being positive is not a method we use to think of what is real and happening now, but a vehicle we use to forget the real and dwell on the illusion of what could be. Granted, to die is to be brain dead, but John, I saw myself dead. I lifted myself from my body, found myself viewing forests and valleys moving with great speed, like an eagle soaring in flight high in the sky. Then there was no flight; it ended."

"Holy shit, Dad! What the hell is that all about?"

"John, I thought you'd agree to listen."

"O.K., Dad, go ahead. What happened then?"

"Well, I pleaded for my life."

"And to whom did you plea?"

"I don't know. I think it was to God. Come to think of it, I just called out and begged to live, for my life was not in order and I did not want to leave my family with all our difficulties.

"I remembered in pleading for life, that Mother would not be able to care for herself and that I did not want to leave you with our business problems."

"Dad, you didn't die! You had a dream! You'd worked hard unloading pallets of ice cream, you were tired, you fell asleep and had a dream. You didn't die; in fact, you are very much alive. It's all a head trip."

"John, who knows. You may be right, but I believe I was going to lose my life and for some reason I was given my life back. Now I fear that Mother's life will be taken in exchange for mine."

"You're gonzo, Dad, out of your head. You're trying to lay a guilt trip on yourself." John rose from his chair, embraced and kissed me, then whispered, "I love you, Dad."

The day was still young, but so much had happened this morning that it felt like two full days had passed.

I remained silent as John drove to the hospital.

I felt terrible, guilty for having created a head problem for John because of what I had said to him.

Turning my head slightly, I glanced at him. He seemed to be normal. I closed my eyes, removing from my mind the thought and feeling of guilt, and experienced the sensation of having done this before. I struggled to understand the dejá vu, wanted to ask it a question, but the sensation quickly faded. Was the Hartsville experience a premonition, a visualization of what would happen this weekend, this morning after Mother's Day?

CHAPTER 2

THE RELATIVITY OF LOVE AND DEATH

D'ANN'S TORMENTED FACE expressed sympathy as she moved to embrace me.

The hospital waiting room had changed dramatically. It was now full of flowers, showing off their colors, emitting a fragrance of love.

"What's happening, D'Ann?" I asked.

"The nurse just left," she said. "Mother is doing well, so far, and they should have her in the intensive care unit in a couple of hours."

"Mother's been in the operating room for over three hours; what's taking so long?"

"I don't know, Dad," she said, trembling. "I am frightened for all of us." We held hands and sat next to Fulvio.

Fulvio and I looked at one another sadly, as if to say, "I just don't know; I can't understand it."

A respected restaurateur, he was owner of Fulvio's Continental Restaurant on Hilton Head, noted for its fine cuisine. Whenever President Ford visited the island, Fulvio was his chef during his stay.

D'Ann had met Fulvio on a sales call to his restaurant while working for our family's business, Masterbrand Distributors.

Sampling the quality, character, and creamy smoothness of Famous Ice Cream impelled Fulvio to go to his freezer, pull out all ten tubs of his ice cream and throw them in the dumpster.

He fell in love with Famous Ice Cream and with D'Ann. He chased her all over Hilton Head. For a year and a half, on a weekly basis, he sent a dozen long-stem roses to D'Ann at our business office.

D'Ann, a contemporary Ms., appreciated his maturity, sensitivity, thoughtfulness and the persistent expression of his love, so she accepted his proposal of marriage.

I called over to John, who was sitting alone, thinking. "Let's go for coffee."

"No thanks, Dad. We just got here. Why don't you sit and read a magazine."

"I can't. I'm going for a walk. I can't stay here any longer."

The beauty and fragrance of the flowers and plants Despina's friends had sent reminded me that she was still in the operating room. Thinking of Despina and this tragedy whirlpooled into a mélange of thoughts slightly diminishing my hold on reality.

My appreciation of the flowers turned into resentment. The image of a funeral home occupied my mind.

Wandering slowly through the hospital corridors I witnessed things I had never before seen. Nurses, doctors and volunteers were in constant motion. Who volunteers time and effort to a hospital, when all around you there's tragedy?

"Hi, Mr. Jonas," said a pleasant little lady.

"Hi."

"Don't you remember me? I gave you a cup of coffee this morning. I hear Mrs. Jonas is doing well. How would you like another cup of coffee?"

I was happy to hear that, for I hadn't heard anything about how Despina was doing.

"Oh, yes, I would love a cup."

"Come with me." I followed her to a tiny office with a desk, two chairs and an urn of hot coffee. "Black isn't it?"

"Yes, please. Thank you. May I ask you a question, Ma'am?"

"Oh, don't call me Ma'am. My name is Evelyn. What would you like to know?"

"Evelyn, everyone here has been so very kind to my family. I thank you very much. Do you work for the hospital?"

"Oh, no, I volunteer four times a week."

"How many volunteers are there?"

"There are about forty of us working all hours of the day and night."

"How long have you been doing this?"

"About five years. Ever since my husband passed away."

"Oh, I am very sorry."

Pausing, I looked at her face and saw an elegant lady, hair combed back in a bun, brown eyes, reddish complexion. She desperately wanted to comfort all who entered the hospital.

The antagonism and resentment I felt when I arrived faded. I was becoming appreciative of all the work that volunteers did.

I thanked Evelyn and continued my walk through the corridors. The early morning hospital odor had given way to a new fragrance. I was being acclimatized to the hospital environment, both physically and mentally. Physically, I could not leave; mentally, my observations of doctors, nurses and employees caring for people in need impressed me. My level of compassion rose, and I promised myself that one day I, too, would be a humanitarian.

Despina was in surgery for eight hours. Finally a nurse informed us that Despina was now in the critical care unit, and we could visit.

We followed the nurse into a room and rushed to Despina's bedside, John and I on one side, D'Ann and Fulvio on the opposite. We waited for Doctor Higgs to arrive.

Despina's head was bandaged, and there were tubes going into her head. Respirators and other formidable life-sustaining apparatus were in place.

"Is she conscious?"

"Dr. Higgs will explain everything," the nurse said in a trembling voice.

When Dr. Higgs arrived, he looked tired.

"It's been a long day," I sympathized.

"I know. Let's step into the corridor," Dr. Higgs said. I motioned for John to follow. "Mr. Jonas," the doctor continued, "You'll be pleased to hear that all went well in surgery. The blood that was pressing on the brain has been drained."

"Great!" I whooped. Then, "No damage to the brain?"

"Dad, let Dr. Higgs finish," John said.

"No damage, and no more pressure on that side of the brain. But I was unable to clip the blood vessel. I could not find the aneurysm. Perhaps in three or four days, when the draining of fluid and blood from her head has slowed down, I can go back into Despina's head and search for the broken blood vessel."

There was a moment of silence. I looked at John quickly, then at the doctor. "Dr. Higgs, let me understand. You're telling me that Despina must have another operation?"

"Mr. Jonas, I could not find where in Despina's brain the blood vessel had burst. She is still bleeding. We need to watch her carefully. The tubes bandaged to the back of Despina's head are to allow the fluids to drain, hopefully stop. Then I will go in again and search for the aneurysm. Remember, the blood vessel has to be clipped or she will continue to bleed."

Dr. Higgs excused himself and I thanked him, wondering how on earth he was able to physically survive the many hours of brain surgery, the most delicate of operations, day after day, year after year. But above all, I wondered how my lovely lady survived it all. John and I returned to the Intensive Care Unit in silence.

I took hold of Despina's hand and prayed for her well-being. My head fell forward, my eyes closed, and I drifted.

"Despina, now that we're in South Country, I'll teach you the Appalachian Jig."

"How are you going to do that?" she asked.

"I don't know, but if you keep waking me up in the morning by blasting country music into my head, I am going to make you dance the Appalachian Jig."

"There's no such thing," she smiled. Have some coffee."

"Oh yes there is, and if there isn't, there soon will be, 'cause I'm going to make it up. Then one day, after it's gone to my feet, I'll dance the Appalachian Jig up and down the streets of Hilton Head."

"George, learn to appreciate the real life stories and poetry of country music."

I took her into my arms and, whispering, "I love you, woman," danced her around the kitchen table.

I looked at her lying there in a coma. Her beautiful face, her beautiful person, lay still. I pressed her hand into mine hoping for a response. There was none. D'Ann was begging her to wake and be well. Fulvio cried. John was speechless and broken-hearted.

The nurse went about caring for her. The lights dimmed and death hovered over her.

Our love, combined, is a greater force than death. The powers of our subconscious minds provide us with a will greater than death's. We as a family will overcome this intrusion, and without thinking, I asked the nurse, "After they clip the aneurysm, how long will it be before I can take her home?"

She paused in her efforts with Despina and raised her head to look at me, her face filled with compassion. She moved toward me, reached out to grasp my hand, and pulled me slightly away from Despina's bedside. I felt the warmth of her hand, felt her pulse beating.

"Mr. Jonas," she whispered, "sometimes it takes months to recover from surgery like this. They haven't yet found the aneurysm, and if Despina has to go back into surgery, there may be further complications. Most of the time," she said, seriously concerned, "patients don't make it."

She pressed my hand. "I am very sorry," she said and left the room.

"Dad! Dad!" D'Ann called. "Mother moved her eyelids while I was talking to her. She heard me. She moved her eyelids, Dad! She heard me!"

I rushed to D'Ann's side, embraced and kissed her, then I leaned toward Despina. Touching her face, I whispered, "Despina, Despina, Sé Agapo Poly Poly." Her eyelids did not flicker. I was disappointed but she'd just come out of surgery; it was too soon. D'Ann must have imagined it, I rationalized. I took my daughter's hand and said, "D'Ann, Mother did move her eyelids; perhaps tomorrow we'll see more."

She bent over her mother, crying, and I moved to the far corner of the room, my thoughts heavily burdened by what the nurse had said about possible further complications.

The corner of the room where I stood gave me a perfect view of Despina and her bedside. Colored lights from the electronic monitors cast rainbows onto Despina's face. The lights flickered, sending forth a light beam that penetrated the drapery of darkness, but only slightly and very briefly a fragment of a moment in time. The repetition, however, gave to my eyes a sense of light. A shiver of fright went from the base of my spine up to the roots of my hair. Standing partially hidden behind a fold of darkness was a strange image.

Then it spoke, its voice familiar to me.

"Your eye caught the sense of my being from the flicker of light."

"I noticed you at once. I believe I've met you before," I whispered. "It might have been recently — or beyond remembrance. Why are you here?"

"Your lack of regard for love has brought me. For years you have taken Philo for granted. Despina's need for your companionship went unfulfilled."

"That's not true," I exclaimed. "How can that be? I have always known love with Despina, and I have loved her as she has loved me."

"Did she not sit alone on the white sands, waiting, wanting you to sit by her side, so she could see and hear all that you saw and heard?"

"That's not fair, Sir. I devoted the past five years to developing a new business. I'll admit I should have spent more time with Despina, but don't accuse me of not loving her! Since my youth I have studied the philosophy of love."

"Examine your thoughts," said the image. "For the last ten years and more your love was incomplete. Have you forgotten what makes love whole? Although each component of love is separate and independent — to truly know love you must bring Agape, Eros and Philo together as one."

I was no longer listening. Anger had overtaken fear. "Who are you? I'm not afraid of you. My will is strong and my thoughts are deep. With my will, that of my children and the powers of our subconscious minds, Despina will heal. She will live."

"Gaze upon her beauty now; adore her presence now; for it may be your everlasting image of Despina," the voice said. "I'll leave now, but do not think of me as evil. I am the Omega of life."

"Death!" I shuddered. "Is it you?" Why was the voice so familiar to me? And what did death know about love? I asked the question out loud: "What do you have to do with love?"

"Alpha, the beginning of life, is love. Omega, the end of life, is death. Between love and death is a breath called time — a perception called life."

The door to the intensive care unit room abruptly opened. The lights when on. A new nurse came in and politely asked D'Ann and I to leave. The drapery of darkness had disappeared and with it the image.

"Dad?" asked D'Ann as she approached me. "What were you doing standing in the corner all alone?"

"Just thinking, D'Ann, just thinking."

"You looked like you were talking to the wall."

On leaving, Fulvio suggested that we all go to the restaurant. His chef had been asked not to leave until his return. Although it was 10:45 p.m., the chef would prepare something for us to eat.

I remained silent as John drove. It was a black night. When there is no light reflecting from the moon, the island darkness is truly dark, very black. People who are afraid of the dark are really afraid of the unknown. What they cannot see into, they cannot know. A distant traffic light faintly lit the night. I watched the darkness change as the green, yellow and red colors of the approaching light altered the black of night. Shades of color originated from the center and extended outward until consumed by the darkness. As we passed the traffic light, the black strengthened until all light was gone, except what glowed in my mind.

There a ball of light remained, white and familiar. It frightened me. I knew this light. I had seen it earlier, by the lagoon. I shook my head to get rid of the light in my mind. I could not shake it.

"John," I called out, "are we there yet?"

"Not yet, Dad. Just relax, we'll be there soon."

My eyes closed. I watched the light in my mind begin to fade, and felt better. No longer was it a flash of white, but something into which I could really see. Within my brain, within my head, within me, I could see.

"We're here, Dad."

"Good." But I continued to sit in place. I felt drained of all energy, like a battery losing the power of its cell.

John came around, opened the door and helped me to my feet. He knew I was experiencing something unusual. I was no longer strong. A strange weakness possessed me mentally and physically. I felt small, spiritless and melancholy.

As we entered the restaurant, I noticed the table had been set. A bottle of wine had been opened, and flowers were arranged as a centerpiece. D'Ann and Fulvio were already seated, waiting for us. The thought of Despina not being with us made my heart pound rapidly against my chest.

I embraced my daughter and we sat down. Fulvio poured the wine, and we prayed for Despina's well being. I raised the glass to my trembling lips, hoping the wine would alleviate some of my despair. I drank the first glass as if it were water. I poured a second glass while the warmth of the first glass of wine was circulating through my body. D'Ann, Fulvio and John were engaged in conversation. I heard the sounds of their voices, but I did not want to hear their words.

I sat in silence, my mind drifting. Was I losing my mind? The bright light, my conversation with Death, my grandmother cooking a dead pigeon, the poetry of nature, the new quiet, the silence, Despina in coma. Was this a normal state of mind for someone experiencing tragedy? Was it normal for death to teach love?

Were Despina to die, then I too will die with her, for I would not want her to be alone. We will die together as we lie together. I'll hold her in my arms, her lovely head upon my shoulder. I'll draw her naked body against mine, press against her for the tender reminder of her femininity. In this manner, together, we shall die.

"Dad, go easy on the wine," John said. I looked up, realizing I had poured myself another glass of wine. How many was that? I had lost count. Had I eaten?

"George, are you all right?" Fulvio asked.

"I am fine; it's been a long day is all. By the way, what is today's date?"

"It's the eleventh of May," Fulvio said.

"Eleventh of May, 1987," I repeated, to document the date in my mind.

"It's almost midnight," D'Ann said. "We'd better call it a night."

"Yeah, Dad, we'd better get some rest. We have an important meeting tomorrow at 9:30 am," John said.

"I'll be in top shape for tomorrow's meeting, don't worry. John, today is the day after Mother's Day, isn't it?"

"Yes Dad, it is."

"Good night all," I said, and John and I left.

Upon arriving home, I played a tape of *La Boheme.*

After spending a few minutes outside with Savannah Lady, John left.

I went into the bedroom, fell on the bed, and lay alone, all alone, without my best friend, for the first time in thirty years.

I closed my eyes. The arias played on, and I fell asleep, a heavy sleep. After awhile, I rose from my tired body and floated. At first, I thought I would fall. I put my hands by my side for support, then realized that my hand motions could move me. Each time I thought of a place I had been, I found myself immediately there.

"Stand under the clock so you won't get lost, and I'll find you," Despina said. Our meeting place was the Biltmore Hotel, a popular meeting place for New York socialites. We sat in a lobby filled with grand sofa chairs.

"George, why did you put this poem in my mail box?"

"I don't know; it was crazy of me."

"Not to me; it's beautiful."

"I'm embarrassed."

"Don't be. I'm very touched by your words and I want you to know that in the short time I've known you, I feel about you the way you feel about me."

"Despina, I don't know what this feeling is, but there's a trembling inside me. I want to hold you and talk to you, tell you all my thoughts. And I want you to tell me all your thoughts, your feelings, about everything. Where can we go to be alone?"

"I don't know."

"Let's get a room here for a couple of hours."

Despina took a deep breath and sighed. "All right."

"Stay here, I'll be right back," I said.

I made arrangements for a room. It was simple. I ordered white wine, club soda, and a bucket of ice.

As soon as we entered the room, I made Despina a wine cooler. I turned on the TV, then I turned it right off. I didn't know what to do with myself. I had known other women before, and loved them superficially, but I really hadn't asked Despina to be with me to make love to her. I just wanted to be alone with her. I felt something different with Despina. She sat quietly sipping her wine cooler as I looked at her; then her eyes caught my stare. Feelings had changed since we left the lobby. The trembling within me had disappeared, and I sensed that Despina no longer felt the love I had written in my poem to her.

"Boy, we're pretty high up," I said as I looked out the window.

"I told my girlfriend Linda about you," Despina said.

"Why did you do that? What did you tell her?"

"I told her that the reason I liked you was that in many ways you were like my father."

She lifted her head and her green eyes hit me with a bolt of love. Dazed, I looked at her. Her long golden brown hair was parted in the middle, the rolling waves pinned back, allowing her hair to fall behind her ears and drape her shoulders. Whenever she smiled, her right cheek rose a little higher than her left, sensuously lifting her tender lips. Her eyebrows were full; her eyelids rested on top of her green irises and her eyes expressed an empathy that melted me. I tried to gain my composure.

"You told Linda that you like me because I'm like your father? Hey, I'm no crazy Greek philosopher. What did Linda have to say anyway?"

"Linda said I was foolish to get involved with you."

"What? Why is that?" Looking out the window, I wondered what people thought about when they jumped.

"Linda said that she didn't see any future in it. You're only nineteen years old, working, still in school."

"What did *you* say?"

"I told Linda that you were very mature for nineteen, that you had lived in New York on your own since you were sixteen."

"What else did you tell her? Did you tell her why you liked me?"

"Well, sort of."

"What did you say?" Despina hesitated. "Tell me!"

"I told you, George!"

"Yeah, I know, I'm like your father."

"I told her I liked the way you think and I like your kind of character."

"What did she say to that?"

"She said that I was silly to get involved with someone who had a hole in his sweater and no money in his pocket."

'No Money,' reverberated in my head. "I've got money; I've saved two thousand dollars the last couple of years."

"Not that kind of money, George."

"What kind of money are you talking about?"

"George, private school girls and New York debutantes marry into money, marry into families with money."

"Is that what they taught you in that private school in Maine? Besides who's talking about getting married? I'm too young to get married!"

"I am not implying we get married." She stood and walked toward the door. "I'm leaving."

"No, don't go," I said. "It's Friday and I don't want to be alone this weekend."

I pulled her tall slender body from the door. My eyes fixed upon a sadness that gave her an inner beauty.

I sat her down on the sofa, leaned over and gently kissed her lips. My hand went up and under her hair to the back of her head.

I pressed her head to my lips again for a firmer kiss.

"George, don't!" She pushed me away. "I am four years older than you."

"So! Now I am immature?"

"No, I don't mean that."

"Well, your being four years older doesn't bother me. I've made it with women twenty years older than me."

"You've had other women?"

"Yeah. Did you think I was a virgin? And what about you?"

"We girls are taught not to throw ourselves around. But you, you're so young," she said.

"Here we go again. I don't want to hear about my age. Besides, we didn't come up here to make it with one another. We came up here so we could talk. Christ! Can you imagine if I were to touch you? Your crazy Greek father would get out his butcher knife, chase me all over the country, and kill me."

"My father's not crazy. Don't keep calling him a crazy Greek. He's highly intelligent and a very educated man."

"O.K., I'm sorry. Do you like cowboy movies?"

"Well, I've seen a few."

I turned on the TV, found a western and flopped on the bed. "Despina, come lie down and watch this cowboy movie with me. It's great,"

She pretended that she didn't hear me. I paused, looked at her, then called again, "Come over here woman, and lie down with me."

She shot up from the sofa, lithe femininity in perfect form, and punched me.

"Don't you ever talk to me like a Greek mountain man, ever, ever again! Understand?"

I grabbed both her hands and pulled her upon me. Her

shapely body, tightly packaged into her Lord & Taylor dress allowed just enough room for my leg to fit between her legs and feel the tightness of her thighs. The contour of her body was exciting and her fragrance intoxicated me. Despina's full breasts pressed upon my chest. Our lips met and we kissed with a passionate energy neither of us could stop. The cowboys kept shooting at one another. Our bodies moved to the rhythm of their gunfire.

"George, I think we should stop," Despina said.

"You're right," I said, but I continued, removing her clothing one fashion piece at a time.

My hands caressed her naked body, awakening the woman within the virgin. My lips fell upon her tenderness.

"George, George, what are you doing?" she breathed.

"Don't talk," I whispered.

Her eyes closed, her head fell back. Sweat created slippery streams that lubricated our naked bodies and increased our passion and eroticism. "George, George," Despina said. "Live in me forever."

"Forever, Despina, forever," I said.

My lips drew love from her breast, and in passionate madness I reached the inner depths of her soul. A bright white light lit the pure consciousness of our minds, and a new love was born.

My eyes opened slightly to early morning of a new day.

Heavy-headed from the wine the night before and out of habit, I rolled over to Despina's side of the bed in an effort to embrace her and whisper 'Good Morning,' to cup her tender breast and kiss her on the neck as I had so many times before.

Instead, I embraced a hairy ape and cupped a dog's wet nose.

Stunned, I opened my eyes and sat up. Savannah turned over, and we looked at one another. Her beautiful head fell to her paws, her eyelids lifted, her brown eyes questioned me, and as my heart sank I realized Despina was gone.

"Oh, Savannah," I cried. "Mother is at the hospital for a few days. She'll be back soon." I stroked the top of her head.

Savannah's brown eyes responded in eloquent sadness and deep concern.

I looked out into the bedroom yard and saw the heat rising to greet the day.

The beauty of the island was captured in the flowering court-yard, the poetry of nature.

We walked into the yard, but I could not hear the harmony of sounds. All was still. A new quiet, silence, and the absence of something else, what, I could not tell. The sky was so high, it seemed there was none. There were an unusual number of birds, but no melodic calls, no choir-like hymns, no chanting psalms, no celebration of morning. Birds were resting on the limbs of big old trees. Four strange white birds, larger than cranes, were silent in flight and appeared motionless against a nonexistent sky in a stillness of flight.

Savannah Lady whined as she sat by my side. Turning to Savannah, I looked at her beautiful intelligent face, and said, "I feel naked, Savannah, and very much alone. Mother is not here and I feel her absence. There are no kaw-kaws, hoot-hoots or singing birds. There is no sky, no wind on my face. I am without character this morning, but I don't feel the despair I felt the night before. At the same time, Savannah Lady, I feel a comfort, an inner joy. It must be because you sit by my side." I bent over and we kissed.

"Uchie!" I screeched. Her wet nose and lickerty-lick tongue

slobbered my face. "Savannah, who ever taught you how to kiss?"

"Hey, Dad!" John called from within, "you better shower. We have an appointment this morning and you need to call John McPherson to confirm that he's coming to this meeting. It's six o'clock now. Hurry! I'll make the coffee."

Upon arriving at the office we learned that Emily, our administrative manager, had opened the office at six in the morning. She had been in touch with our delivery route people who were located in five distinct areas of South Carolina; she had prepared documents for our meeting with representatives from national headquarters of the Famous Ice Cream Company and our attorney, John McPherson. Emily embraced us, offering sympathy without words.

She briefed us on the previous day's sales activity, as we enjoyed coffee together in the conference room. Emily had come to work for us a little over two years earlier. I remembered how astonished I was by her manner of speech. I hadn't expected a southern born African-American who had never been out of the South speak such a clear, cultured English. Since she was also practiced in data processing, I'd hired her to be our administrative manager.

Angelic and still youthful despite her thirty-six years and a face that revealed a lineage of southern hardship two centuries old, Emily was not only efficient but beautiful.

As she continued her briefing, I politely asked to be excused. I looked at my watch; it was a few minutes after seven o'clock. That left two-and-a-half hours until the meeting. I refilled my cup and carried it to my office.

I heard Emily say, "Let him be, John. He needs to be alone."

Sipping on my coffee, sitting back in my chair, feeling alone, but safe within myself, I looked out the window at the pink and rose-colored flowers of the hibiscus shrub. I could hear Despina call, "George, come see the beauty and splendor of the sun reflect on this simple flower. George, come with me this morning and see the glow of color come up from the ocean and meet the sky. We'll walk with the dolphins and see them smile at us."

"Oh, God!" I whispered as I turned away from the window. Despina had for years been asking me to share in her inner ecstasy, to hear the harmonies of the island birds, to see the beauty of the setting sun upon the island marsh, but I had been deaf to her call and blind to her vision.

All I had ever wanted to do was build a family business for my son and daughter. I stood up for a moment, then sat down again. I was becoming uptight. Despina's only fifty-three years old, for Christ sake. There's no way she will die; she's too young to die. We need to spend time together. In a panic, I picked up the phone, called the hospital, asked for the nurse in charge of the intensive care unit and asked about Despina.

"She's doing just fine," she said and hung up the phone. What the hell is wrong with people, I wondered. I call to find out how my wife is, they tell me she is doing fine, then hang up on me. I caught myself growing angry and paused, reflected, and realized there was little else she could have told me.

I called the hospital again. "Dr. Higgs, please," I said.

"Dr. Higgs is at his office this morning; you can reach him there," the operator said.

I called his office. "Dr. Higgs, George Jonas here,"

"Glad you called, Mr. Jonas," he said. "I saw Despina early this morning, and she's making great progress."

"Is she awake?"

"No, she's still in coma. It takes time, Mr. Jonas. But the good news is that the bleeding and draining of fluids has almost come to a complete stop."

"You mean there's no more dripping from her head?"

"That's right, as of this morning."

"What about the broken blood vessel?"

"That's the next step. We need to give the healing process time, then we'll see. I'll see you at the hospital in the afternoon."

I closed my eyes and prayed. "Oh, God, thank you, thank you for saving Despina. Thank you for giving us another chance to be together. I'll give Despina the rest of my life, every minute will be hers, only hers. Thank you, dear Lord."

I sat back in my chair, placed my hands behind my head, looked out the window and thought back to where it had all begun. Reston Virginia was a new community just outside of Washington, D.C. I had been commissioned in 1978 to establish a paper-products service business on the mid-eastern seaboard.

With a budget to work with and ample expense money, I was entrusted with enormous responsibility.

I packed up family and dog and hustled them off to a new home in Reston, Virginia. John remained in Boston to continue his studies. Three and a half years later, having worked twelve to fourteen hours a day, six days a week, with the help of the staff I had developed a new service industry.

Vacation time had come around, and although I needed a month I felt I could only be away from business for two weeks.

I promised everyone — Mother, D'Ann and John, that we would have two weeks without business. Late one afternoon, in discussing the vacation with Despina, I made mention of Mexico.

With a burst of anger, Despina called out, "No more Mexico! No more Acapulco! That's all you know, George. The last time we went to Acapulco you almost drowned the kids. Then you almost got us killed in the mountains in a safari jeep, at a time when rebels were kidnapping Americans. You almost drowned diving for octopus, and if it were not for John and the young Mexican guide, you would be at the bottom of Acapulco Bay."

"Yeah, Mother," my lovely daughter D'Ann confirmed, "and remember what Daddy did on the pyramid?"

"What did I do on the pyramid, D'Ann?"

"That was a real doozie," said Despina. "If you think the children and I are going to climb the pyramids with you again so you can call out to God like you did last time, humiliate and embarrass us, you're crazy. Besides, the children are older now, they won't stand for that kind of behavior."

"I never did that, Despina."

"You did too!" D'Ann and Despina cried in a single voice.

"You made us climb to the top of the pyramid. Then it started to rain and while everyone else was rushing for cover and running back down the pyramid you began screaming and calling out to God. And don't you dare deny it," Despina warned.

"But, Despina my love, why climb a pyramid if not to talk with God?"

"To yourself, George, to yourself. Not to stand in the pouring rain with your arms stretched out screaming, 'I believe in one God! Father of the Universe! Oh, Infinite Intelligence,' and dancing, doing a Zorba the Greek dance and singing, 'If I were a rich man, lah-de-lah-de-lah-de-dum' on top of the pyramid in the goddamned rain. There we were — somewhere in the middle of Mexico with people watching and asking us if you were in your right mind."

"Just imagine, Despina," I responded, "if the pyramid were Egyptian and came to a point, rather than Mayan with its a flat top, my insanity might have gone right up their butt." She was not amused, so I threw up my hands and said, "All right, you decide where you would like to vacation, and we'll go. I won't say a word."

"You mean it, George?" Despina asked. "You really mean it?"

"You better make Daddy promise, Mother. You better make him promise," D'Ann advised.

"Promise me then," said Despina. "Promise you won't say a word, you'll just come on vacation, no matter where we go."

"I promise, Despina. I truly promise," I said. "Honest."

I hugged her. The softness of her cheek and the fragrance from her hair reminded me of expressed love from an earlier time. While holding Despina in my arms, I kept staring out the kitchen window. There, in the backyard, I saw myself dancing on a pyramid in the rain; only this time I was not alone.

Nine Indians of an ancient civilization appeared dressed in ceremonial robes. Ribbons and ornaments crowned their heads. Each wore a necklace of gold-carved Indian faces that reflected the colors of the rainbow as they danced around me. A man in a black robe with red and gold patches stopped and faced me. Brilliant colors flashed from his robe and clashed with one another to create electricity that united and formed a bright white light around him.

The rain continued to fall around us but not on us. Only the sun beamed down on top of the pyramid.

A call echoed through the curtain of rain. "George, are you coming down from that pyramid?"

"George, let me go. You're squeezing me."

"Oh, I'm sorry," I said, releasing Despina from my embrace.

"What were you thinking about?"

"Something in the backyard reminded me of Mexico, and I

remembered your calling me to come down from the pyramid," I said.

"I told you, Mother. Dad's got Mexico on his mind for our vacation."

"No I don't, D'Ann."

"George, you promised me," Despina said.

"That's right and I'm going to keep my promise."

D'Ann and Mother looked at one another and smiled. "O.K., what's up? What's going on? Have you made plans for our vacation already?"

"Tell him, Ma," said D'Ann. "He made a promise and he has to keep it, so tell him."

With great pride and a big smile, Despina said, "We are going to South Carolina for our vacation."

"South Carolina? What the hell is in South Carolina?" Then I learned that Despina had contracted a three bedroom townhouse for two weeks in Sea Pines Plantation, South Beach, Port Harbour, Hilton Head Island, through a travel agent. I kept my promise; no more wild expeditions, just good behavior.

The beauty of Hilton Head Island so overwhelmed us that a year later we talked about the possibility of moving there.

Then one day it happened. I asked Despina if she would like to spend Washington's birthday on Hilton Head. "We'll stretch the weekend to four days, fly down, leave on Thursday, come back on Tuesday."

"I'd love to," she said, "but with one modification: no planes, just trains. I want to go by train."

As a child living in New York's Greenwich Village and attending the prestigious Little Red Schoolhouse, Despina and her dad had traveled to Maine by train for vacation. Later, she took the train to the Oak Grove School for Girls in Maine. On holidays they would travel with friends to Greenwood Lake in upstate New York by train. All her travel was by train during her school years.

"Despina, I haven't been on a train in years. Washington, D.C. to Savannah, Georgia by train takes ten hours. It's going to be a suffering, bouncing, stop-and-go experience," I said. She remained silent. "It's dangerous to travel Amtrak high-speed trains these days. They forgot to lay new rails to handle the increased train speeds, Despina. They use the same rails the Irish, Negroes and Chinese laid in the early years of our developing nation. How can you expect me to travel 110 miles per hour on railings 150 old that were designed for old chug-a-lug steam engines?" I said.

Despina smiled. She said nothing, simply smiled, but the gleam in her eye made me give in. No planes, just trains.

That holiday weekend with Despina at the Palmetto Dunes Plantation, we decided to change the course of our lives. I would take a one-year sabbatical from work. Despina would leave her position as manager of the boutique. We would pack up, sell off, and move to Hilton Head Island, like pioneers in covered wagons in search of a new land.

We were ready for a new experience. Despina was forty-seven years old, and I was forty-three. It was the right time to break from our lifestyle and search for tranquillity in a new environment. We were ready to change our lifestyle, to hold hands and walk the beach and just be together.

I thought of Despina softly walking onto the deck of the townhouse so as not to disturb a squirrel chomping on a nut. She paused, looked out at the landscape of tall pines and blossoming bushes that lined a fairway of pure green, and said, "I am going to love it here."

CHAPTER 3

AN UNJUST ENRICHMENT

"MR. McPHERSON IS HERE," Emily said, knocking lightly on my door.

"Be right there." I sipped on the cold coffee in my cup. I felt awkward, weakened by my thoughts about moving to Hilton Head. Taking hold of myself, I greeted my attorney. "John McPherson, thank you for coming."

"It is my pleasure, George. I was telling John a moment ago that South Carolina has some tough laws about distribution, but first I want to say how truly sorry I am to hear about Despina."

"Despina is in a coma, Mr. McPherson, and we don't know what to expect."

"Well, I pray all goes well. Shall we cancel this morning's meeting?"

"No, I need to resolve this problem. What's your opinion about this letter Famous Ice Cream sent us?"

"It sounds threatening, but let's hear what they have to say."

John McPherson was a genuine Southern gentleman; he was not only educated, but cultured. He was soft spoken, but beneath the soft southern accent was a tornado. Injustice summoned from him a display of rhetoric that could lift you out of your chair. If you were not honest with John McPherson, Esquire, you would surely regret it.

Emily entered the conference room. "Mr. Peterson and Mr. Bradshaw are here."

"John, will you greet them and have them come in here?"

"Sure, Dad." When John returned with guests in tow, introductions were exchanged. Mr. Peterson expressed sorrow for Despina's illness, and I thanked him.

"Gentlemen," I said, "I have asked my attorney, Mr. John McPherson, to be present today, for I did not appreciate the tone of your recent letter. Your letter states that if we don't cease requesting a distributorship agreement with the Famous Ice Cream Company, you will stop sending ice cream products to us and put your own company trucks into South Carolina.

"Now, let's go back just prior to January of 1983. During the months of November and December of 1982, Mr. Bernie — then Vice-President — and you, Mr. Peterson, gave my son and me permission to negotiate the purchase of a distributorship from Gourmet Foods of South Carolina.

"I informed you and Mr. Bernie that if I were to purchase the rights to distribute Famous Ice Cream products from Gourmet Foods, I would need a distributor agreement with Famous Ice Cream Company. Mr. Peterson, you, then told me that Famous Ice Cream never had any agreements with its distributors. However, now that Popular Foods Company has purchased Famous Ice Cream, you said that agreements would be forthcoming within six months, and that I should go ahead with the purchase of the distributorship for Famous Ice Cream products. Again, I expressed my concerns to you, indicating that although I was purchasing the distribution rights from Gourmet Foods, I would need something in writing from you. I asked you for a letter of appointment. Do you recall that?"

"I do."

"Then, in January of 1983 you sent me this letter authorizing and appointing me as a Famous Ice Cream distributor. You and Mr. Bernine were aware that we never had any prior frozen food experience and we were going to have to invest large sums of money in freezer trucks, freezers and plant equipment.

"Is that correct?"

"Well, yes."

"Four years have now elapsed and I am still begging you, the man who authorized me to purchase the Famous Ice Cream distributorship from Gourmet Foods, for the distributorship agreement.

"Annual sales at the time of purchase, according to your figures, were sixty thousand dollars total within the State of South Carolina. Here are the documents supporting these facts that you gave me at the time of purchase. Today, our sales are twenty-two thousand dollars per week, over one million dollars per year. Our capital investment is three-hundred twenty-five thousand, but now, when I ask for my distributorship agreement, you, Famous Ice Cream Company, and Popular Foods find reason not to forward it to me."

Mr. Bradshaw said nothing. Peterson looked stunned. Were they beginning to realize their game plan was unethical?.

I looked directly into Mr. Bradshaw's eyes. His face registered deceit and duplicity and Peterson, once the strong man, was now a puppet, fearful of losing his job under Popular Foods new management regime.

I turned to my attorney. "Mr. McPherson, can Popular Foods Company cause us a problem?"

He cleared his throat. "As I said earlier, they are going to have to pay for your distribution. The State of South Carolina has laws protecting distributors after moneys have been invested and years of sweat equity have been poured into a business. It would be against equity and good conscience to terminate your distributorship and may be cause for actual and punitive damages."

Peterson's face turned red as I continued, "Gentlemen, you know, one of the stories that really touched me was about how Simon Goldberg, owner of the Famous Ice Cream Company, was an honorable man who never believed in contracts with his distributors and never had a problem with them.

"His word was his contract, good as gold. An honorable handshake, a single word, *'Mazeltov'* — 'good luck' in Hebrew, was all that was needed, in his opinion. Mr. Bernie, his successor, my son and I have honored that tradition. You tell us we are the South Carolina distributors, but Popular Foods refuses to put it in writing. You continually ask us to service more markets, yet you deny us promotional help and credit. We, John and I, with investment moneys from others, paid for the expansion. Famous Ice Cream has never offered to help us. Now after all these years, you deny us our rights and what is just.

"Is it Popular Foods Company, the new owners of Famous Ice Cream, or the foreign group that has just purchased Popular Foods Company that's putting the screws to two little guys in the State of South Carolina?

"Gentlemen, it has been four years and we have built a successful distributorship. Tell me why we can't get a distributorship agreement from Famous Ice Cream Company?"

Mr. Peterson stood and said, "George, you and John deserve a lot of credit. You built a business from polyfoam containers to four freezer trucks, from annual sales of sixty thousand dollars to over a million. I don't see why we can't extend you more credit and promotional help. Don't worry about the distributorship agreement, just keep increasing the sales volume."

"Does this mean we'll get our agreement?"

"We'll work on it, George."

We exchanged good-byes and they left.

"Dad, you and Mr. McPherson must excuse me. I am going to the hospital to see Mother." I knew John wasn't running away. I could see the burden of concern on his face regarding our business.

"I'll join you there shortly." I said. Turning to the attorney, I asked, "Mr. McPherson, what do you think?"

"It's difficult to say, George. Peterson sounded sincere, but he may well be under pressure to deny any promises to you. I heard that Famous Ice Cream bought out the Florida distributors."

"Yes, about six months ago, and they recently forced the distributor in Georgia to sell out to them."

"What do you mean by forced him to sell?"

"Jerry told me that he received a call from Popular Foods Corporation in Chicago requesting a personal appointment. He agreed to meet with them, and several Popular Foods officers and a vice-president in charge said to him, and I quote: 'Jerry, we're not putting a gun to your head, but we want to buy your business and if you don't sell, we are going to put our trucks in Atlanta, open distribution here, and put you out of business.'

"Jerry consulted an attorney in Atlanta and was informed that because there was no a written distributorship agreement, he should agree to Popular Foods' demands. That's why I'm insisting on my distributorship agreement."

"When did this happen?" Mr. McPherson asked.

"Oh, about eleven months ago."

"Do you know how I can get in touch with Jerry?"

"I'll have Emily find his home address for you," I said. "Mr. McPherson, Popular Foods bought out Florida because they were too big to steal or push around. They forced the Georgia distributor to sell to them. Now they are looking at South Carolina and possibly North Carolina. Geographically this would give them control of distribution for the entire Southeast region. That's their game plan. I'll sell to Popular Foods but only for the right price."

He shook his head. "Companies like Popular Foods will start to send you negative letters of your performance and put a squeeze on your line of credit. They will delay shipments to you and cause you internal office chaos, if they are planning to force you out of your distributorship. Watch for these signs, George; if they take your customer base, it would be an unjust enrichment."

"How can they take our accounts! We opened, sold, and developed these accounts!"

"I know." He shook his head, walked toward the door, and waited there for me. We shook hands.

"Thank you for coming. I am most appreciative."

"We'll talk later in the week, George."

Afterwards, Emily and I sat over coffee and briefly discussed business for the day. "A Mr. Patrick's been calling you."

"What did he want, Emily?"

"He didn't say."

"Did he leave a number?"

"No, he said it was personal and that he'd call back."

All our employees were carrying the ball, taking care of business. Emily was running the show and our route men were doing a fine job. They loved Despina and gave John and me time to care for her. I thanked Emily and left for the hospital.

The car moved slowly. I looked down at the speedometer. Twenty miles per hour. I wanted to go faster, the car also wanted to go faster, for it sometimes choked as I drove back roads, but for some strange reason, we stuck at twenty miles an hour. The back roads of Hilton Head reflected the glory of the old South. I kept returning to the meeting with Bradshaw and Peterson, even as my eyes registered the landscaped beauty outside and, simultaneously, my concerns for Despina in the hospital.

"Peterson sounded sincere," I said aloud as the car continued to drag along, but why did he and Famous Ice Cream send me that threatening letter warning me not to ask for a distributorship agreement? "We are entitled to it, for God's sake. John and I have slaved for four years, poured all our money into the development of Famous Ice Cream distribution, and now that we're successful, they threaten us with cancellation."

They can't cancel our distribution, I said to myself. I bought and paid for this distribution. My thoughts ran as rapidly as the car moved slowly. A couple of cars passed, one driver me giving me the finger and another guy calling me a jerk-off, but I just smiled at them as they angrily sped forward.

I decided to find the bill of sale with Gourmet Foods, along with the original purchase agreement and general warranty. We had those documents. We'd bought the piece-of-nothing distributorship with authorization and permission from Famous Ice Cream and built it into a major frozen food distribution network. They couldn't cancel shit! We owned it. All of it. This was America!

The warmth of the day and the heat from blood rushing through my veins brought a sweat to my brow. The perspiration ran down my forehead and into my right eye, irritating it. I emerged from the back roads and found myself in mad traffic moving quickly around the Sea Pines circle. A new determination encouraged me. I straightened myself in my seat — stood tall mentally — and became more aware of the things around me.

I'll call Emily and have her look for those documents. I saw Rock's Party Store ahead. I'll pull in and call Emily; in fact, I owe Herbie money for the Jameson's Whiskey I bought yesterday. Was it yesterday? Yeah, man, it was yesterday. It's only been a little over twenty-four hours since all this happened.

The big old oak tree looked much larger than it had yesterday, its limbs stretched much farther from the trunk than before. It seemed taller, too. Brown and gray with hanging Spanish moss that gave character to the surrounding commercial area. As always black men were hanging around the big old oak, standing 'round its proud base, as if belonging to the tree. The limbs embraced them offering shelter from the rays of the sun.

This land, this giant of a tree, may not have belonged to these men, but the men, the native men, the black man, belonged to the tree, belonged to the land, nature in balance.

A black man called, "George, George." It was Abraham. "How is Mama, George?"

"I don't know. I'm on my way to the hospital now. The doctor said that she's doing better. "Would you like some coffee, Abraham?"

"Surely would," he said. "Surely would."

"Here, you go get two coffees; make mine black. I'll go see Herbie and I'll meet you back here." I gave him money for two coffees.

"Need to tell you, George. I found the Lord!"

"What?" I said.

"I found the Lord!" Abraham said.

"O.K! You get the coffee and we'll talk after I see Herbie."

Herbie wasn't there, so I left the money with the clerk and went back outside.

Abraham and I had become friends over the years. Sometimes he would walk into our offices, ask to see me, and we'd sit and talk. He'd tell me about his boxing experiences.

"I'd've hit him with a right cross, a Sugar Ray Robinson right cross," he'd say.

"What's a right cross?" I'd ask.

"George, you fake a left to the face, then you quickly step to the right with a hard, straight left to the gut and blow the man over, then come straight across with a right to the side of his face." I would tell Abraham of my experiences at the Whitehall Hotel in Harlem. I liked talking to him about my teenage years in Harlem. I wanted Abraham to know that I was a regular guy and that he could talk with me.

Relating to Harlem allowed Abraham to be at ease with me, even though his only Harlem experience had lasted for only two weeks. Being Southern born and bred, two weeks was all he could take in Harlem.

He would roll over in laughter. "I don't believe it. A little white boy with all those black dudes at the Whitehall Hotel in Harlem, playing poker and cello. They're mean motherfuckers, man!" He slapped his knee and keeled over with laughter.

His light brown face darkened from the rush of blood to his head, and I wondered whether he'd be as distinctive and as handsome if his face were white. Three deep lines ran across his forehead telling stories of hardships. His nose was long, his lips were thin. He was a white man with brown skin.

"They took care of me, Abraham. We were family. They watched out for me. I had three close friends: Jocko, Jimmy Brown, and Babalou."

"Wha' cha' all do for work?"

"We unloaded bananas from freight cars at the Bronx Terminal Market. I wasn't always a philosopher, Abraham. I'm just becoming one now, thirty years later."

"Me too, George. I'm just becoming a philosopher like you now."

"You know, Abraham, we could never be philosophers today if we didn't have the tough times and experiences of yesterday."

"Ya man, and we can still kick ass, can't we?"

Arriving back at my car, I found Abraham waiting. We sat in my car and sipped our coffee.

"What's happening, Abraham?"

"I found the Lord, George."

"Great!"

"Ah'm going to church now. I ain't been in years, but when I stand in church, I get a new kind of feeling. A feeling of love. Ah'm learning ta love and I found the Lord Jesus."

I sat quietly for a moment staring into my black cup of coffee.

"I'm happy for you Abraham. Don't let that feeling leave you. I need to find the Lord too. I need to find the Lord so I can ask him, 'Why?' I need to ask him what the hell is going on. Why is all this happening to me and my family? I need to ask him, 'Why is Despina in the hospital? Oh, Lord! Tell me, Lord!'" I called out in an arrogant and accusatory tone: "Why have you now sent two unethical bastards to steal from us our invested moneys and rape us of the years we spent laboring. Tell me, Lord! Why?"

Abraham was aghast. "George, you can't talk to the Lord in that way. He'll never give you anything you're askin' for."

"I'm sorry Abraham, forgive me; it's not right of me. I'm just out of my mind now. I gave more than four precious years to a business I may lose. I took those years away from Despina. I feel I've sacrificed her, that I've placed her high on a pyramid as an offering to the gods."

"What's you talkin' 'bout George?"

"Christ, Abraham, I don't know what the fuck I'm talking about. It just came out of me. I have to go to the hospital now; we'll talk again later."

"George, I'll pray for Mother," he said, and returned to the crowd of black men hanging around the big old oak. A tall man, he walked proudly. Rags of three colors hung from his left back pocket. His pants and shirt were worn. He turned and waved good-bye. His distinctive profile stood out from the group of men.

Abraham's face stayed with me as I drove to the hospital. His saying, "I found the Lord," echoed in my mind.

I kept in pace with the heavy traffic, talking out loud to myself, occasionally hitting the steering wheel. Each periodic bang inflicted slight pain, reminding me that I was driving a car, although my mind was elsewhere and continually leaving. I was so removed from my surroundings that I was seeing myself and my environment elsewhere.

After driving around I found the road to the hospital located deep in a wooded area far off the main road. I couldn't remember driving there. I only recollected hitting the steering wheel. Had I experienced different states of mind, different realities at the same time? Signs directed me to a familiar parking lot. I parked the car and then sat still. I noticed the remaining coffee in the holding tray. I sipped at it and tried to remember driving to the hospital. I had clear memories of talking to myself, visions of past discussions and past experiences, right up to leaving the office. I even visualized conversations taking place after the meeting.

I know I physically drove a vehicle, yet I could not remember driving. Was this a conscious act of a subconscious state? A parallel universe? A thought process which was not real? Surely the reality, the awareness of driving, was not real.

I poured the rest of the cold coffee on the ground and raised my head. I hesitated walking into the hospital for fear of what I might be told. The familiar big bold red letters, **EMERGENCY**, gave me a dreadful feeling.

Two double doors led into the hospital, two levels high but stretched out. The parking lot was full of cars. I wondered why. I closed my eyes. I wanted to pray. I needed to pray. But I also resented the need. God was not my favorite person this morning, this moment. He had caused me many difficulties these last 24 hours, and I was torn with feelings of resentment and anathema.

My head fell forward again. I began to cry inwardly and tried to hold back the tears, but soon they were flooding my eyes. "Forgive me, God!" I whispered. "Forgive me, for I did not mean to curse your heavenly Father's name, nor to harbor in my heart a resentment of your glory. I am ashamed to call upon you, God, for I feel undeserving of your favor. It has been years since I have acknowledged your presence or have thanked you for our lives. Now with heavy heart, a mind about to explode, a body tired, I further offend you by placing the blame of my difficulties on you. Please forgive me, Father. Allow me only to pray for Despina's well-being. I ask nothing for myself. Take all I have. Let the thieves rob me. Take from me your pneuma for I am not worthy of it. End my life. But give back the pneuma that gave life to Despina, for she is worthy of it."

I envisioned myself talking with God as I sat in true silence. I could hear nothing. My thoughts vanished. I felt an inward rush of energy flood my mind. The sensation was the catharsis of my subconscious. I lifted my head and my vision, previously blinded by tears, was cleared by tears. The bold red **EMERGENCY** sign no longer troubled me. I got out of the car and walked across the parking lot with determination and enthusiasm. The unknown, my fear of what I might discover beyond the hospital doors, no longer concerned me.

I challenged the heavy double doors through which I was about to walk. I would find life or death beyond the doors, and I was ready for either. Whatever God willed. I would walk through the doors with my head held high, with pride, with dignity, and without fear.

CHAPTER 4

GOOD MORNING, MORNING GLORY

THE HOSPITAL DOORS automatically opened, as if welcoming me. I walked through and turned to look at the doors. "Thank you," I bowed, showing my respect for the doors, showing as well that I had overcome my apprehension. I could hear muffled laughter from people in the hospital corridors. They thought me funny, so I bowed to the doors again and then to the people laughing before I hailed the receptionist.

"Nurse," I asked, "Why are there so many cars in the parking lot and so many people in the hospital corridors? There are only 15,000 residents on this island."

With a smile, she said, "Yes, but don't forget the 100,000 people who come to visit the island each month. Most of the people here are visitors."

A young mother comforted a little girl who was crying. A jellyfish had stung her. The corridor was lined with vacationers, people on a break from their work life. Beautiful young college girls were assisting a friend thrown from a jet-ski or para-sail. Letting go, I called it. Everyone was on vacation just letting go, mindless of the cost of careless play. I observed them, stared, looked at their faces, especially at the faces of the women. I was looking for someone in the hospital, someone I was to meet.

Slowly walking, watching, being watched, drifting mentally,

the renewed enthusiasm and determination I had just experienced was diminishing. I searched for a woman whose laughter was infectious and whose smile was slightly crooked. She had an oval face with green eyes, a suntan, short light brown hair with streaks of amber bleached by the sun. That's what I was looking for, exactly that! I was searching for Despina. I was scouring a crowd of women for *my* woman, for a Despina who was full of life and laughter, forgetting, for the moment, the reason why I was walking through the hospital corridor.

The traffic thinned as I neared the elevator. Signs on the wall at the end of the white corridor pointed the way to other medical units. The door to the elevator opened with a thump like a beat on a bass drum. Two nurses in white uniforms, one holding an antenna-like rod with two suspended bottles filled with fluid attached to a little old lady who was lying on a roller slab, the other guiding the cart. I could not look away from the green-eyed nurse holding the rod with the swinging bottles.

She caught my piercing stare as the collision of thought, like cosmic rays smashing into one another made her look upward. I dropped my gaze and it fell upon her breast, particularly the one on my left, her right. A perfect breast held in place by thin white clothing. The nipple rose against the garment, offering to my imagination a moment's delight, sensuous pleasure. She must have felt my gaze or my thoughts for she lowered the arm holding the rod with the swinging bottles to level the playing field of her bust. Her name tag introduced her as Laurie Cartwell, R.N., and as I was about to address her the door of the elevator opened with a thump. Nurse Cartwell turned her head as our eyes met again. Her light-brown hair was pulled back from her face and tied neatly behind her head. Her eyebrows were full and there was a sadness in her eyes.

"Nurse," I sputtered, standing in the elevator door like a dummy.

"Yes?"

"Ah, nurse, ah, which way to the critical care unit?"

"Straight ahead. Are you a doctor?"

"No, I'm not."

"You were on the wrong elevator. Are you all right, Sir?"

"Yeah, I'm fine. Thank you," I said as she walked down the opposite corridor with her entourage. I wanted to run after her so that I could tell her my thoughts but, instead I slowly walked the other way toward our assigned waiting room.

What would I have said to the nurse had I stopped her? Would I have said I was looking for a Despina? Would I have told her I liked her green eyes because Despina has green eyes? Or would I have said, "Dear Ms. Nurse, your green eyes are beautiful. I gazed upon your bosom because their fine form intrigued me. I thought of my passionate lips giving warmth to their nipples and my face feeling the softness of their feminine magnificence." Or, "Dear Ms. Nurse, permit me to fall upon your bosom for I have need to cry like a newborn. I need the warmth of your breast to provide me with a sense of security, I need to draw from your nipple energy for my life."

Which of these thoughts are truly me? Could it be that I was man and child at the same time? Was this anticipated grieving or a call out to Despina in a different state of mind?

I continued walking, pausing with each step, dragging my heavy feet, slowing my forward motion in an attempt to slow down time. But I knew that even as the seconds would pass into minutes, I would pass through these corridors in concert with time.

No one was in the waiting room, so I went to the critical care unit. D'Ann, John, Fulvio and, to my surprise, Fulvio's mother, Mama, had assembled around Mother's bedside.

D'Ann was sitting by her side reading to Mother as she lay motionless. Every word was spoken with love, and the room trembled with it as D'Ann attempted to penetrate Despina's deep state of unconsciousness. Her voice was like a javelin quivering as it sped through the air. D'Ann's eyes acknowledged me, but her determination to enter Mother's mind was all that mattered.

Fulvio stood by D'Ann's side, a hand resting on her shoulder, giving comfort and assuring her in a quiet way that all would be well. Fulvio, by nature, was a quiet man, except, of course, in his restaurant and especially in the kitchen. There, he was a mad genius, a bilingual, creative, pan-throwing chef of chefs with the movements of a modern dancer and the voice of Pavarotti. Mama stood on his right side, her hand softly caressing Despina's calf. Chanting prayers in Italian, she held a crucifix in her other hand.

I felt slightly resentful. I had in no way envisioned an exhibition of Catholic or Greek Orthodox religious ritual. Despina and I became Protestants five years after our marriage. The furthest thought from my mind were rites of any kind, before or after death. I looked at Mama praying. She was small, half the size of Fulvio. Her stamina, youthfulness and determination were incomparable. I went over to Mama, put my hand on her hand holding the beads and whispered, "Forgive me, Mama, for my thoughts. Please Mama, pray."

She did not understand me, nor was what I had whispered for her ears or anyone's. It was for my conscience alone. Mama said something in Italian. I could only understand the word, Georgio. She proceeded to tell me something, and I listened attentively for a moment, then said, "Grazia, Mama, Grazia." I kissed her on her head and walked over to where John was standing.

A nurse's aide entered the room and advised us that we would have to leave in ten minutes. It was time to care for Mother, but Dr. Higgs would meet with us in about an hour. I was hoping everyone would leave, so I could be alone with Mother, so I could whisper into her ear words of love, but no one left. "There will be time later," I thought. I took hold of Despina's hand, closed my eyes and silently begged. "Oh, Father in the heavens above, give back your spirit, your breath of life. Let Despina be well." I pressed her hand, looked at her stretched out motionless in bed and thought, "What is this phenomena of life and death? I must understand it further, learn more of life in order to comprehend death."

My eyes shifted with my thoughts to the far corner of the room where the strange image I had seen the night before had emerged from the darkness. But now there was no darkness, no image. If only the image would appear, I might understand all thoughts of life and death that were incomprehensible to me. The image would bring light to the darkest corner of my mind. I would have answers to all my questions. I decided to search for a similar experience that night.

"You must leave now," instructed the nurse's aid, her voice bringing me back to reality. In the waiting room, Mama, Fulvio and D'Ann sat together. John drifted to one side of the waiting room, seeking solitude. I felt his distance, so I sat on the opposite side of the room, away from the sunlight that beamed through the windows.

I knew as soon as I entered the waiting room fragrant with plants and flowers that I had to sit away from the windows, though surely not away from John. I was not going to allow my-self to experience my grandmother again by standing or sitting anywhere near the sun's rays. I was having enough head trips with an unknown image as it was, and I needed to eliminate unnecessary thought processes and as many abnormal happenings as possible.

A feeling of insecurity came over me, however. Why was John sitting alone? I needed him, his strength, his love, his shoulder to cry upon. I wouldn't have, for I was the father and he the son. I should have comforted him. Should we not comfort one another?

I looked over to where John sat business-like in deep thought. His face expressed profound sadness, and his handsome head weighed heavily on his broad shoulders. He picked up a newspaper and placed it on his lap and was about to read when he hesitated and looked across the room at me. I caught the seriousness of his expression, but I could not interpret the thought. Normally, I could translate John's facial expression, but not this time. Knowing the pure agape he had for his mother, I wondered whether my son resented my being up and around and very much alive.

Would he prefer to have Mother up and around and very much alive while I lay in a coma awaiting death? Would he make such a distinction? I knew it would be best, and to everyone's advantage, for me to pass on first. I was well insured. I had always anticipated passing on first and isn't it easier to let go of a father than a mother? I wondered whether the thought of parental preference had crossed John's mind.

The waiting room was comfortable. The arrangement of sofas and chairs divided the room into quarters, allowing for a degree of privacy. I looked over the sofa, past the flowers, to view D'Ann in Fulvio's embrace. Her head rested on his chest near his left shoulder. Mama sat on his right, holding her prayer beads and crucifix, chanting out loud, praying in Italian. My eyes shifted back to D'Ann. Her beautiful young face was in torment, pained by the dilaceration of love from her soul. A mother removed from a daughter's love is a separation of agape from psyche; like a simple piece of paper torn in two, so was her love for Mother torn in two. Torn from life to share with death, torn from the present to suffer the past, torn from the real to experience the unreal, she would struggle with images and visions of what once was present but now was past. Holding hands, sharing the warmth of love between a mother and daughter, walking on the greens of a fairway, observing the beauty of the reflections from a setting sun, in a glory of companionship — no longer would this be the present but the past, no longer the real but the unreal, a memory of love to age and fade away.

I observed this pain and torment on the face of the young mother-to-be, wanting life for her mother just as she was giving life to her child. Her head rested on another man's shoulder, on Fulvio, her husband, and not on my chest, I, her father. When did the reality of her love transfer to another man? It wasn't so long ago when I held my little girl in my arms and she wept tears for simple reasons. When did she grow up to be a woman? In what unreality of our lives did this transition take place?

I walked over and took D'Ann by her arm, leading her to an area of the room where we could be alone.

"D'Ann, I'm so proud of you," I said. "You've been a caring and loving daughter to your mother. You've been Mother's best friend. You spent time with her when I could not."

"Oh, Dad! Right now I feel I was nothing to Mother."

"That's not true." D'Ann looked sad and beautiful. She dressed well whatever the occasion. Mother had taught her correctly about clothing.

"Simplicity is beauty," Despina would say.

D'Ann's eyes were glassy from crying. Her thick reddish-brown hair, complimented by her brown jacket, gave color to her pale complexion. I took her hand; her palm was wet from trembling and from fear. "Dad, I can't wait to take Mother home so I can really love her up, and make up for all the arguments we've had."

"D'Ann, you can't have love and friendship without an occasional difference of opinion. Feel fortunate that you've been so close to Mother. You're Mother's proper little lady, and as soon as we get her out of this hospital we're all going to love her up and care for her. You'll see D'Ann. All will be fine."

"Oh, Dad, I need your strength."

"D'Ann, I need your strength too."

"Stai zitto! Stai zitto!" Mama called out to Fulvio.

"What the hell is that all about, D'Ann?" I asked as Mama continued yelling at Fulvio in Italian. "You better go help Fulvio."

"No, let them have it out. I won't get between Fulvio and his mama."

"Well what's it all about?"

"Fulvio told Mama to stop chanting and praying 'cause it was driving him crazy. Mama then flipped her lid and told Fulvio to stop talking — *Stai zitto, stai zitto*, shut up, shut up."

"Look at Mama go! I think she's going to haul off and wallop Fulvio."

John got up from his seat and took Fulvio by the arm. "We're going for coffee," he announced, and left the room with Fulvio.

D'Ann went to comfort Mama. I followed. Mama was crying and talking in Italian, holding her prayer beads tightly in her thin, strong hands. D'Ann put her arms around Mama, comforting her, loving her, attempting to fulfill her own desperate need for the embrace of her mother.

"D'Ann, why is Mama so tormented? She only met Mother a month ago."

"Mother's not the only reason Mama's been praying. Poor Mama's been through hell recently. That's why Fulvio had Mama come over from Milan to stay with us for a couple of months."

"What kind of hell has Mama been through?"

"If I tell you, you can't let Fulvio know that you know."

"I won't let on, I promise."

"It's been over twenty years since Mama's husband died."

"Yeah? So?"

"Well, a couple of months ago, the priest and the man who takes care of the cemetery and Antonio, Mama's nephew, all went to where Mama's husband was buried and dug him up."

"Why in hell did they do that?"

"It's a custom in some parts of Italy, that after you've been dead for more than twenty years, they remove you from your grave, clean off your bones and give them to your family."

"That's fuckin' barbaric!"

"They need the ground for someone else to be buried in. But wait, that's not the whole story, that's not the real reason Mama's upset."

"Why then?" I asked, embracing Mama, loving her frail small person.

"Georgio, Georgio," said Mama, continuing to chant words I could not understand but only felt.

"Go on D'Ann, tell me the rest."

"Well, as Fulvio tells it, the priest started praying and the two men began digging — "

"D'Ann, you mean the gravesite had not yet been dug open?"

"Dad stop! Will you let me tell you what happened?"

"O.K., go ahead. 'The two men began diggin' "

"After an hour, with Mama crying and praying and the priest reading aloud from his Bible, Antonio climbed out of the grave while the caretaker stayed down and opened the coffin. 'Antonio, all the meat is off the bones,' he called up and took the skull from the casket and threw it up to Antonio. Antonio dropped the skull, and it rolled down to Mama's feet. She flipped out, went berserk with crying and praying. Antonio picked up the skull and held it as Mama placed her hands on her husband's head. Antonio threw the skull back into the grave, but the man collecting the bones from the coffin didn't catch it. It bounced all over the casket, and Mama really went bananas. The caretaker climbed out of the grave and started punching Antonio and screaming at him. Meanwhile, Mama's going out of her mind 'cause they disrespected her husband's remains."

"Well, what the hell was the priest doing all this time?"

"He was reading special prayers from his book."

"What happened then?"

"The two men, still yelling at each other, took hold of Mama's arms and started to walk her down the slope to her home. Can you imagine what a sight that was? Two men with baggy pants yelling at one another, with Mama in the middle having a fit, while the priest followed reading prayers aloud."

"What a morbid experience." I attempted to reflect upon the past, in order to realize a part of my forgotten life, but my mind couldn't let go of Mama's terrifying experience.

I was at a loss. I felt abandoned and frightened. I was lonely and needed to be embraced, wanted to embrace someone.

If only I could go to Despina, be alone with her, lift her from her pillow, hold her in my arms, squeeze her tenderly and whisper words of love to her what a glorious moment that would be for me. I wondered if a father's loss was greater than the children's loss? If one loses a beloved mother, is the loss greater than if a father loses the mother of his children?

Why did I need to weigh the loss? Does pain wrenched from one heart weigh more than pain from another? Was my pain heavier because I bore the torment and pain of my children along with my own?

Their loss, a mother so divinely loved; my loss, the mother of my children, a life-long companion, a woman I truly loved, a woman I lived with for over thirty years. With this feeling of loss, this floating, empty, lonely feeling, came tears for my children, knowing their pain and torment, their feeling of loss. I wept their tears and felt their pain.

No, a father's or mother's feeling of loss is not greater than that of the children; it's just that the parent absorbs and devours the suffering of the children in addition to his or her own. But how did the collective mental anguish I experienced compare to Despina's pain, her loss, her suffering? Why was I crying over my loss? Should I not be crying for Despina's loss? I tried to reason with my feelings but could not. Something had gone wrong in my life, and I wasn't quite sure what it was.

John and Fulvio returned. D'Ann joined her husband. Mama sat alone praying. I couldn't help smiling.

"What are you smiling about?" John asked me.

"Oh, nothing."

"Come on Dad, share it. I need a smile too."

"I was just thinking about the time our Miss Dee took us out for an early Sunday dinner."

John's face lit up, his eyes gleamed, and I knew right then, that split second, that he had left the present to reflect upon the past.

He stood up. He was six feet tall but seemed ten feet high from where I sat. He paced the floor, holding that smile. I noticed a quality and elegance in his stride reminiscent of his mother. "Tell me how it happened."

"Well, it was on a Sunday, and Mother wanted to have dinner at this restaurant she had heard about. After an hour of driving we found the place. Of course you and D'Ann were much younger."

"How long ago was that Dad?"

"About ten years ago. You and D'Ann were still in high school. The waitress came over to our table.

" 'What will you have?' she asked.

" 'We'll all have the buffet,' I said.

" 'No! I don't want the buffet; I just want a salad,' Mother said.

" 'Despina, have the buffet or a lobster,' I pleaded.

" 'No, I just want a salad. You and the children have the buffet.' "

"Mother loves salads, doesn't she?" John smiled.

"Yeah, salads kept Mother in shape, John, but she also loved to pick the goodies off everybody's plate. Anyway, the waitress said, 'Three buffets and one salad, right?'

" 'Right,' I said.

" 'Sir, we do have a very strict policy.'

" 'What's that?' I asked.

" 'Any member of a party not ordering an entree is not allowed to eat off another's buffet plate. You see, some people come in, pay for two and try to eat for four.'

" 'Well, Miss, that's not what we're all about.'

"John, do you remember how the three of us had scrumptious buffet plates of lobster and shrimp and salad, while Mother just had her salad? Then she forgot the rules of the house and, out of habit, she took a hell of a good looking shrimp off your plate. The waitress saw and ran over to our table with great speed. 'You all have to leave the restaurant!' she fumed.

" 'What?'

" 'Your wife took a shrimp off your son's plate.'

" 'Despina, did you take a shrimp off John's plate?' I asked.

" 'Yes, I did, and what's this nonsense about one shrimp?' Mother asked.

" 'Well, you'll have to leave,' the waitress said.

" 'We all have plates full of food,' Mother replied; 'we have had two rounds of drinks, and if you continue with your threats and invasion of our dining privacy, Miss waitress, we will leave — and without paying the bill.' "

"What happened then?" John asked.

"Mother sat very proud, silent, and elegant as she waited for a response."

"What did you say, Dad?"

"Nothing, Mother told me to stay out of it. I just felt the wind from her long strand of pearls.

" 'I'm sorry,' said the waitress, 'That's our policy.'

" 'That's it, George. Take the children, we're leaving,' Despina said.

" 'Ma!' cried D'Ann.

" 'George, take the children and please wait in the car,' Despina said. We left, Mother remained and went to talk with the owner. Moments later she returned.

" 'What happened Ma?' we said.

" 'The waitress misinterpreted the restaurant policies. There are people who take advantage, but you don't pounce on a family and ask them to leave unless it's abusive and they're really trying to rip off the restaurant. The owner apologized for the waitress's poor judgment and inexperience, and asked us to stay' Mother said.

" 'How's that?' I asked.

" 'I told him who I was,' she said

" 'Hey Ma! Who'd you tell him you were?' D'Ann asked.

" 'Yea, Despina, who'd you say you were?' I echoed.

" 'I told him I was Miss Dee of the Camellia Room, and that I knew and dressed his wife.' Despina said.

" 'Miss Dee! Miss Dee of the Camellia Room, Wow!' We teased Mother all the way to another restaurant."

"Hey, Dad. You know what?"

"What's that, John?"

"Why didn't you take charge of the situation? Why did you let Mother handle it?"

"Remember, John, Mother created the problem. When she asked me to stay out of it, I did. I never stifled your mother. That's what I love about Mother — she's a woman's woman. Independent. I love her person."

"I don't think I would have handled it that way."

"How would you have handled it?"

"I would have told Mother to back off. I am the man, and I am in charge."

"Funny, funny, funny. You would never talk to Mother that way."

"I am not talking about Mother. I'm talking about a wife. If I were married, I'd tell my wife to keep quiet, and I'd take over."

"Wrong! John, have you ever heard me refer to Mother as my wife?"

"No. I've always wondered about that, Dad."

"Whenever I introduce Mother, I refer to her as Despina.

When we go out to parties, friends' homes, social events, I say, 'Mr. Davis, this is Despina, Mrs. Basset, this is Despina,' not, 'Hi Mr. Davis, I want you to meet my wife.' "

"What's wrong with 'My wife, Despina?' " John said.

"Introducing or calling a woman a wife takes away from her person makes her secondary, reduces a woman to an adjunct."

"C'mon, Dad, you introduced Mother as Despina 'cause you didn't want any of the ladies to know you were married," John jibed.

"Not so! I want women to stand tall. I see women, beautiful women, and I don't mean just looks — I mean character — being beaten down by men. Beer drinking, bottle guzzling 'chewtabac' men. A man who loves a woman should feel he's walking with a Venus or a queen. Even if he can't measure up to being a king, a man's manner toward a woman will be noticed, and if it's respectfully correct, he'll be king to his queen," I said.

"When I marry I am going to make sure that she's not an independent motor-mouth like my sister."

"John, D'Ann's a liberated, beautiful woman. She carries herself well. She's analytical in thought. She's considerate and polite, and she's a humanitarian."

"Yeah, sure! She's analytical in thought all right. I call it blabber-mouth dialectics."

"And you? What are you, John? A macho man?"

"No, I'm not a macho man, but when I tell a woman to sit, I expect her to sit."

"Then don't marry a woman, John, marry a dog. Where did you get that kind of attitude? That's not you; your mother and I didn't bring you up that way. Don't ever let your mother hear you talk like that!"

A pleasant and refined man, Dr. Higgs expressed sincere concerns for us, and his efforts to save Despina brought me closer to the man within the doctor. We all gathered around him to listen as he updated us on Despina's condition.

"The draining has diminished greatly," he said. "However, I am concerned about not having found the aneurysm. The bleeding will not stop unless we clip the blood vessel. We must go back in."

"Dr. Higgs," I cried out, "We're right back to page one, right back to where we started."

"That's correct."

"And when do you want to perform this operation?"

"With your permission, within the next day or so, depending on the draining of fluids from her head."

"Do all you can to save Despina," I told him. The rest of the family remained silently in shock.

"You may go in and be with Despina now," Dr. Higgs said. "I believe the nurses have completed caring for her."

So, again, we were all standing around Despina's bedside gazing at her motionless body. Mama assumed her position with prayer beads and crucifix in one hand softly stroking Despina's leg with the other while whispering prayers. Fulvio stood tall and firm, his hand on D'Ann's shoulder as D'Ann spoke lovingly to her unconscious mother.

"Mother, I know you can hear me. I love you! We're all here with you. Please open your eyes just a little bit. Squeeze my hand just a little bit. Please, Mother. John's kissing you on the cheek and telling you he loves you. When you come home next week, John and I are gonna take you country dancin'. Fulvio's got a very special bottle of wine for you to go with your favorite salmon dish. Mama wants to take a long walk with you, and she's been praying for you to get well. Dad's been crazy and he won't be himself unless you come home. He loves you, Mother."

D'Ann moved closer to Mother's ear. Her tears fell on the pillow. "And Mother, I just want you, my mother, my beautiful mother, I want you. Please wake up so you can be with me and the baby. Imagine Mother, I'm going to have a baby girl."

John leaned over to his sister and said, "D'Ann, you are a very beautiful person, and I love you very much."

I was left standing aside, feeling alone, having lost my place in the adoration of Despina. Should I push everyone aside and fall upon Despina sobbing louder than the others? Of course not. I must stand aside and allow the children created within her and emergent from her to arch over her, so that they might have what could be a final opportunity to be with their mother.

"Death," I thought, "you are inspiring a love within me I never felt before. Never have I known such an ultimate expression, not just of pain and torment but also of love's emotion. You are an open wound in my heart. Love's emotion is my morphine, and I struggle to apply its application through thought. Although I am momentarily relieved, I heal not."

My children continued to solicit their mother, begging her to respond. I stepped backwards quietly and made an exit into the corridor. Dr. Higgs was with a nurse reviewing a medical chart. As the opportunity presented itself, I approached him.

"Dr. Higgs, may I have another moment with you?"

"Certainly, let's go to the waiting room."

"Dr. Higgs, brief me again, if you will. I am very concerned about another operation into Despina's brain."

"She is a healthy, strong woman, George, and we have no alternative; we must go in again. If we do not, the bleeding will continue. We must find the broken blood vessel and clip it. I searched all over the side of her brain where she was bleeding, and I could not find the aneurysm. We must find it and clip the blood vessel," he said, a compassionate look upon his determined face.

I knew that Despina was in good hands, but I also knew that should Dr. Higgs fail to find the aneurysm this time around, death would take her. My head hung low. "Dr. Higgs, how did this aneurysm come about?"

"There are a number of ways," he said. "Despina could have been born with it. We also know that Despina smoked more than a pack of cigarettes a day since prep school. Nicotine inhalation along with other chemical gasses from cigarettes can cause the smaller vessels of the brain to become brittle. As one gets older, blood pressure can cause these delicate blood vessels to break, causing blood to flood the skull."

"Dr. Higgs," I interrupted, "I am sorry to keep asking you the same questions."

"I understand," he said, "and I'll do everything I can to keep your very loving family intact."

Distraught and weakened by the excessive mental and physical energies, I had to fuel the thought processes of my mind, for I was feeling a new mood come upon me.

A new presence engulfed me. I was alone in the waiting room — this I knew and understood — but I was also elsewhere. I felt lighter and taller, and white matter was all around me and moving with me. Every man and woman experiences mood swings when a loved one is in a state of being transferred to another universe. It's a normal experience; everyone has to go through it, I thought as I wiped my eye glasses clean.

Transferred to another universe — that's it! We'll all be transferred to another world, another universe, only to be created once again through love. We then pass on again through death, and with each transition a higher intellect and a superior being evolves.

Why was I having these thoughts? There was no time to reason why, for my mind was racing back in time.

There was a wetness upon my face and the fresh fragrance of an ocean breeze. "Uncle Nico, what are you doing?"

"My boy, I am testing the heat of this animal fat."

"But Uncle Nico, you spit in the fryolator."

"That is correct, my boy. Nothing can live in this animal fat, this frying oil, after it reaches its proper temperature. At night when the fryolators are turned off and the animal fat cools, it creates bacteria which can make people ill. Don't concern yourself with my spitting into the fryolator, for as you can see this degree of heat has destroyed all."

I looked into the fryolator and saw the dancing spit evaporate like water on hot oil.

"You see, my boy, now you must save mankind. You must parade the streets of Smithtown, Long Island and educate the public. Tell them that the animal fat with its preservatives clings to their French fries, enters the blood stream and slows the passage of blood to their brain and their heart. They eventually will deteriorate and die. This my boy, should be your concern."

I had arrived at Nick's Ranch Restaurant, far out on Long Island, the night before. This was to be my summer weekend job, out of the city and near the ocean. Nick had hired me to work the front part of the restaurant. Nick's name was really Costas, but he called himself Nick. Nicholas was Costas brother, but I called him Uncle Nico out of respect.

Mr. Mike was Uncle Nick's and Uncle Nico's cousin, and I was to call him Mr. Mike and all three were learned Greek philosophers who talked strangely about familiar things. Each summer Nick would open the restaurant for the beach trade. Mr. Mike lived on the island all year 'round caring for the chickens, goats and peacocks, while Nick traveled back and forth to Manhattan to his other business interest.

Uncle Nico was in his late fifties. He had a beautiful head of white and brown hair swept back to expose a high forehead. He spoke softly with a Greek accent.

Whenever he spoke and whatever he spoke about became philosophical and analytical. This is how my classical education began. "George, my boy," Uncle Nico said, "bring me the two pails that are under the kitchen sink." Disturbed, I went to fetch the pails. He knew that I was repulsed and concerned about his spitting into the fryolators. "Place the pails under each of these spigots, George and we will drain this lard, this animal fat. Then, my boy, I will show you how to clean, thoroughly clean, the fryolators."

I looked up at him with astonishment and he smiled. "Do you think that I spit into the fryolators without good reason?" he asked. I shrugged my shoulders. "Does it upset you?"

"Yes, it does."

"And, it also awakens you, does it not?"

"Yes, it does."

"So because you have a concerning nature and are a fine young man, with the potential to be a humanitarian, I will allow you the privilege of draining the fryolators of all the fat. Then scrub down the grease with this brush and a solution of soap and hot water. Had you not been concerned, my boy, about my spitting into the fryolators, then I would not have bestowed upon you the honor of cleaning the fryolators. Anyone who would not be concerned about another man spitting into the fryolators would be without character and not clean them well. But, George my boy, you are very concerned. Therefore, I know you will clean them well."

I stood there, dumbfounded, trying to figure out what had just happened. If I had showed no concern, he would not let me clean the fryolator, but because I was concerned I was qualified to clean and wash them. I said nothing, trying to understand the logic of the man.

The hot fat poured out of the spigots and into the pails. "This lard is from butchered pigs and cows. It has been melted down, then treated with the worst kind of preservatives," Uncle Nico said as he walked out into the back yard. I followed him.

Nick's Ranch Restaurant was located on the Jericho turnpike between Comack and Smithtown next to the Indian Head Restaurant. With two hundred feet of frontage and fifteen acres for a backyard, the main building had been converted into a restaurant, grill and bar with additional rooms on the second floor. A house with five bedrooms was off to the left, and chicken coops crammed with chickens and little chicks stood about three hundred feet to the rear of the main building.

Uncle Nico gathered loose lettuce leaves and other vegetable scraps and began feeding them to two goats.

"Uncle Nico, what are those chickens all about?"

"George, my boy, my brother Nick was once a professor of Genetics at the Massachusetts State College in Amherst. These chickens are the result of his insane theories on the breeding of fresh laid hen eggs."

I looked at a long row of shack-like dwellings. "Who takes care of these chickens?"

"Who takes care of these chickens you ask? Pete does, Pete

the plumber who plugs for the union." I did not dare to ask him what he meant; I just listened.

"Pete's a graduate student working on his thesis in animal husbandry. He gets up early every morning, runs to the chicken coops and sticks his crooked fingers up the chickens' asses to check for the development of eggs." said Uncle Nico.

"All of them?"

"Yes, all of them. And if you ever hear a screeching rooster in the early morning, you'll know that Pete plugged the wrong chicken," he said.

"Are you also into chickens, Uncle Nico?"

"No, my boy, I'm into words. I'm a poet."

Now I was totally confused. I didn't know what to believe. I went back into the building to tend to the fryolators. Mr. Mike walked by talking to himself.

"Good morning, Mr. Mike," I said, but he did not reply; he just kept talking and walking up and down the galley with a cup of coffee in hand. I tried to stretch an ear so that I could hear what Mr. Mike was muttering about to himself. It sounded like he was counting numbers and reciting the Greek alphabet.

The grease filled both pails. I shut the spigots and went to where Uncle Nico was playing with the goats and sipping his coffee. "Uncle Nico, the pails are filled with grease, and I shall wash the fryolators when they cool. What do you want me to do with the grease?"

"Let the grease cool out here in the back."

"Uncle Nico, Mr. Mike is talking out loud to himself and walking up and down the galley; is he feeling well today?"

"Mr. Mike is a chemist and a mathematician, a graduate of the University of Athens and of Rutgers and Columbia. He is a brilliant man. In the early mornings he speaks to no one but himself so not to waste his mental energies on small talk. He applies his well-rested mind to the application of reason in physics and metaphysics."

"Oh," I said as if I understood, then returned to the grill area near the front yard and began to wash the fryolators.

Standing out in the front yard, looking up at the sky and talking to himself was the frail, distinguished-looking man. I watched him for a moment, then I called out to him. "Mr. Mike, what's up in the sky?" I intended to disturb him, to break his train of thought and bring him back to reality, for I thought he was about to flip his lid, go bananas on me. I didn't really care what was in the sky, but I called again, "What's up in the sky? I have coffee for you."

Mr. Mike walked toward me. For a moment I thought he was angry. "What's up in the sky?" he said, as he took the coffee I had poured for him, "I'll tell you what's up in the sky, George. The heavens are in the sky; my dear mother is in heaven and I often look up and talk to her, for I love her dearly. The infinite intelligence is in the sky and, when my thoughts are transmitted, I am one with the universe."

"What kind of intelligence?" I asked.

"There is no time for talk now, my boy," he said. "Finish washing the fryolators; we are running late with our preparation. Crowds of people will soon be upon us."

"Right!" I said. I rushed to the cash register for a pencil and paper to write down 'infinite intelligence,' so I could research its meaning at another time.

A heavy hand fell on my shoulder. "Dad, are you asleep?" John asked.

"Huh! Oh, no," I responded. "Well, sort of. I was about to fall asleep; I was in a daze. What time is it?"

"It's late, Dad, almost midnight."

"How is Mother?"

"The same, Dad, the same."

"I feel like someone knocked me out, John. Where's D'Ann and Fulvio?"

"They just left. Come on, let's go home."

I struggled to my feet. I felt I had aged. John took me by the arm, and we walked through the familiar white corridors. "John, how tall are you?"

"Six feet and one-half inch," he said. "Why?"

"Oh, I don't know," I said, turning to look at my son, now twenty-five. He had his grandfather Nick's high forehead, his hair swept back like Nick's and Uncle Nico's. "You look like your grandfather, and you walk like him as well."

"How's that?"

"With great pride."

"I love you, Dad."

"Love you too, John."

Driving home, I began to laugh at what I had dreamt when I dozed off in the waiting room.

"What are you laughing about, Dad?"

"Just thinking about how I met your mother and her crazy family."

"How's that?"

"Drive slowly and I'll tell you. I was working for your grandfather at his restaurant on weekends. One day, this girl I thought Nick had hired, was working the cash register. She leaned on it in a most unbusiness-like manner. 'Hey Miss,' I said, 'stop sleeping on the cash register. Stand up straight.'

"She turned and looked at me as if I were a peasant without the right to address her behavior. I was working the grill. It was a busy time of the day. One side of the grill had fifty frankfurters; the other side had thirty hamburgers, and the grease was smoking and dancing on the hot grill. People kept coming, ordering like crazy. Uncle Nico, your grandfather's brother, managed the French fry department, just behind my work station, and his cousin Mr. Mike was at the far end of the galley talking to himself. I don't remember what he was cooking. Anyway, this girl at the cash register irritated me. She wasn't taking in the money fast enough, and every ten minutes she'd leave the busy register to go for a smoke. Well, I just got pissed off at the whole nutty crew, so I screamed at the girl, 'Look, Miss,' I said, 'pay attention to collecting money and stay at the cash register when we're busy, for Christ's sake!' Instead, she left the register unattended and never returned.

"With a little help from Uncle Nico, I managed to get through the busy period. I found Nick in the bar and was going to tell him that we had a problem with the cashier when who do you think was at the bar having a drink with him but this girl. 'Why did you leave the register?' I asked her. Without a word she turned her head away from me, and just as I was about to tell her off, Nick called out from the other end of the bar.

" 'George, my boy, I would like you to meet my daughter.' He came forward and said, 'Despina, this is George. He is going to work the front and supervise its activities.' Despina turned, looked at me, stepped down from her bar stool and left.

"I smiled, then sat at the bar and talked to Nick. 'I am sorry for my daughter's attitude,' he said.

" 'That's O.K., Nick. I can handle it.'

" 'I know you can George.'

"John, I'll never forget the heartbreak on your grandfather's face. 'George, my daughter is really a lovely person. When she was thirteen, her mother and I separated. Florence went on to pursue a career as a concert violinist, and I was too busy to take the time to raise Despina. We shipped her off to a boarding school in Maine. She's twenty-three now, and I am worried about her!'

" 'Does she live here?'

" 'No, she lives in Manhattan with her cousin Melissa.'

" 'What does she do for work?'

" 'She's an assistant buyer with the Allied Stores. She only comes up here on the weekends. George, try to work with her, please.'

" 'All right, Nick,' I said, 'I will.' That whole weekend I kept smiling at her, but she still refused to talk to me."

"Mother must have been difficult then," John said.

"There was a tiny flicker of arrogance within a flame of elegance, all illuminated by beauty and kindness."

"That's Mother all right. Well, what happened? How did you two get together?"

"Two weeks passed, and the second weekend she was on the train to Long Island, sitting alone smoking. It was like in a movie scene. I noticed her and went over and sat across from her. There was a moment's silence. She looked at me, surprised. I looked at her and smiled. Then we both burst out laughing.

" 'Hey Despina, I knew you weren't stuck-up,' I said.

" 'What you mean is that I'm a bitch, don't you?'

" 'Oh, no, I never thought that,' I said."

"As I looked out the window of our fast-moving train, I realized I was moving backwards and, for a moment, it bothered me.

So did the word 'bitch.' Part of me kept looking out the window; I felt something was leaving me along with the landscape rushing past the train window. Another part of me kept looking at Despina, and I had a feeling that she too was mesmerized by the motion of landscape whizzing toward her. I now know how I fell in love with her."

"Sounds interesting. Tell me how."

"Our love was brought about by motion."

"You mean, emotion."

"No, I mean motion."

"The kind of motion you had was in your pants. You had the hots for Mother and you won't admit it."

"John, that's crude."

"Sorry, I didn't mean any harm. O.K. Dad, tell me how motion caused you and Mother to fall in love."

"All right. Now picture this carefully — are you ready?"

"Yeah, yeah, go ahead, I'm ready."

"Picture Despina and me on this fast moving train sitting next to the window, opposite one another. I'm going backwards; she's going forwards. We're looking out the window of the train at the apparent motion of passing scenery. Every so often, we turn and look at each other. Then at one particular moment, our eyes met and our auras unlocked from our bodies and embraced one another."

"What? Let me understand this. Mother's aura and your aura left your bodies, met between you and Mother sitting across from one another, and the auras embraced each other on a moving train, and that's how you fell in love. Now tell me how the auras came to leave your bodies?"

"The auras unlocked because Mother was looking out the window at the landscape coming toward her and I was looking at the scenery leaving me. Motion mesmerized us and when our eyes met, the auras unlocked and embraced. Simple"

"Uh huh, want some coffee?" John asked.

"No thanks."

"Dad, did Mother wear a dress that day?"

"Yes, she was dressed beautifully."

"When Mother sat across from you, did she have her legs crossed?"

"Yes. Why do you ask?"

"I'm just trying to picture your theory on motion and auras."

"Your mother fascinated me. Her face showed she wanted companionship. I could tell she was lonely. She wore a very tight dress and with high heels on she was taller than me. That used to bother me, for I felt that a man should always be taller than the woman he was with. That was just one of my hang-ups back then.

"People always stare at Despina, not because of her beauty, but because her presence created curiosity. I remember getting off the train and extending my hand for her to step down from the train. When I took her hand, goose bumps shivered up and down my back. Moments later, standing in the depot, staring at her, I was still holding her hand. I wouldn't let go. I knew she had a similar feeling about me, too."

"What then?"

"Well, from that moment on, we would try to meet one another on the train to Long Island every Friday. It was all very exciting."

"In what way?"

"I couldn't wait for Fridays to come along. I'd run like crazy to make the six o'clock train, then wobble through the passenger cars searching for her. I'd pretend that my meeting her was just a coincidence, but what intrigued me most was the sensation I felt each time I would meet with her."

"So you did have the hots for her."

"There you go again with the hots, for Christ's sake."

"I'm sorry."

"I know, son, but that's what pisses me off these days. People can't define love. Young people don't know what love is. To them, love is having the hots for someone; a hard-on; it's so one-dimensional."

"Then what was the sensation you felt?"

"Well, try to imagine this, John. Jerking back and forth on a moving train, I saw Despina up ahead sitting alone. Nonchalantly, I moved closer to her. She saw me coming up the aisle toward her. She turned her head and looked out the window of the swiftly moving train, pretending not to notice me.

"I approached her and said, 'Hi!' She turned in false astonishment, smiled and responded with the same 'Hi!'

"At just that point, that moment exactly, an energy-like electrical discharge was felt by both of us. I sat opposite her and felt my heart pounding against my chest. An aroma of flowers, the fragrance her perfume had upon her femininity, alerted my senses. An exultation traveled through me and I was drawn into a magnetic field illuminated by the bright light emanating from her person. That was the sensation."

"For Christ's sake, Dad, I don't mean to offend you, but if that's not having the hots for Mother, what the hell is?"

With that, we both burst out laughing and we were still laughing when we drove into our driveway. Having been left alone for over eighteen hours, Savannah Lady jumped like a crazy dog all over us until we let her out. John suggested we have a glass of wine.

We toasted Mother in a prayer, clinking our glasses, embracing one another. "Get some rest, Dad," John said.

I carried my wine into the bedroom, then I called to him from my bedroom. "That was pure love, agape, an emotion truly felt from my heart."

"Yeah, I know, but don't forget you were nineteen then. You're reflecting upon the past philosophically, thirty years later. What is agape now was the hots back then," John said again laughing.

I sat on the edge of my bed sipping wine and questioning my thoughts. Was my love of thirty years ago created by desire or was it truly a heartfelt emotion? Which came first?

I knew love then. I might have neglected it in later years only to be reminded of its eternal soul from the mysterious visions hidden in a drapery of darkness. But I knew love.

I hugged my pillow tightly and tried to think back to my first encounter with love. My eyelids closed, and I fell asleep, dreaming of a garden of multi-colored roses. They were like maidens bathing in the morning dew, reflecting a glorious rainbow in the warm rays of a golden sun, singing hymns, giving praise in their full bloom. I appreciated their forms, perfect and imperfect, as they charmed me into their field of fragrance where my sight fell upon one.

What creative force from my inner mind acknowledged that one? I looked upon that flower, deep into her eyes, into the center of her bloom. My subconscious instructed my heart to send blood rushing through my being, enriching my mind, giving me the energy to reach into my very soul, enabling me to feel the God-given emotion called love, agape. Whereupon, my voice trembled. "Come, oh precious one, come. Let me adore you."

Out of the garden of love, I boarded a bus from West 4th Street to 96th and Madison. "Did you enjoy your dinner, Despina?"

"George, I've had a most delightful evening. I'm not one for opera but when the bartender played music on the liquor bottles and the waitress sang arias from various operas, I was moved. And, my scampi was great. I'm very impressed," She said.

I smiled, pleased that I had impressed Despina on our first dinner date. Luigiano, the head waiter, and Tony, the night manager, treated me like a king when they saw me walk into the restaurant with Despina. I had never enjoyed such recognition, and it felt great. Though I wasn't a student, I was always welcome to eat a bowl of pasta and calamari with the opera students. Luigiano and Tony, the owners of Bianca and Margaretta's Restaurant, were very kind.

"Do you ride?" Despina asked.

"Sure do," I said, then paused. "Ride what?"

"Ride horseback."

"I guess so. I've never been on a horse, but I love to watch cowboy movies, so I'm sure I can ride."

Despina smiled, and looked out the window of the bus. I felt stupid about my response and looked for the signs of indifference she had shown me the first time I met her at Nick's. Instead, she turned back and said, "I'll teach you how to ride, George. Next weekend, up at Nick's. There's a stable two miles from the restaurant."

"Uh, O.K.," I said. "You know, you're quite different from the Despina I met at your father's restaurant."

"That grease hole turns me off. The only reason I go up to Long Island on weekends is to see my dad. I don't want to be alone in Manhattan on weekends. Besides, I only go up during the summer months. Dad closes down in September and works at his business in the city."

"What other business does your dad have?"

"He and his cousin John operate checkrooms in nightclubs like the Blue Angel and the Village Vanguard, and in hotels like the Biltmore and the Commodore. One day I'll take you to meet my friends from school. We always meet at the Biltmore Hotel."

"Your dad said you were a buyer. What do you buy?"

"I'm an assistant buyer for Allied Stores. I buy dresses and shoes."

"Where's your mother?"

"Somewhere in Europe playing the violin. What about you? I understand that you work for American Airlines; what do you do there?"

"I punch holes in flight manuals."

"What do you mean?"

"Well, I work in the publications department at LaGuardia field. After they print manuals, I drill holes in them and fit them into a binder, but that's only for the next two weeks. I'm being transferred to a different position."

"So you'll be working in town. Where do you live?"

"On 86th and Fifth, just ten blocks from you."

"How can you afford to live there? Do you live with someone?"

"No, I have my own place. It's very nice and I only pay twenty-five dollars a week."

"How's that?"

"Well, Mrs. Andrews, who owns the building, teaches at City College. She's putting a Greek English Lexicon together. I catalog for her and research the etymology of words, especially Greek words and some Latin."

"You know Greek?"

"Not like your father, but I had five years of Greek and two years of Latin. A Jesuit schooling, although I'm not a Jesuit."

"No wonder my father likes you."

"You went to school in Pennsylvania, didn't you?"

"Yes, after they threw me out of Columbia. I finished at Lycoming College. You're originally from Boston, aren't you?"

"Yes."

"When did you leave?"

"I left home early and went to Williamstown in Massachusetts. Lived with a cousin, and worked at Tanglewood for the Boston Symphony Orchestra."

"You did!"

"Well, it was just a summer job."

"I didn't know you were a musician, too."

"No, Despina."

"What do you play?"

"I don't play. Well, I do, but I don't."

"Oh come on, tell me. I'm all excited. What do you play?"

"I play trumpet."

"You do? Oh I love it! Will you play for me sometime?"

"Want to hear me play the blues?"

"Now, on the bus? But you don't have your trumpet with you."

"No, but I got my hands."

"Your hands? Really? On the bus?"

"Yeah, why not?"

I placed my hands together and started to trumpet blues into the hollow palms of my hands. Despina cried with laughter. "Oh, you look so funny! Play it again; that was good."

"I play saxophone, too. Want to hear?"

"Sure."

"I play piano too."

"Oh, come on now. You don't play three instruments."

"No, I play five."

"What are the other instruments?"

"Ham and cheese sandwiches."

"What on earth are you talking about?"

"Despina, I worked as a sandwich maker in the kitchen at Tanglewood. I would lay out fifty slices of bread at a time, slap on a slice of cheese, then come around again and slap on the ham, then put the other slice of bread on top and bag the sandwich."

"But you said you worked for the Boston Symphony Orchestra."

"I did. My paycheck read Boston Symphony Orchestra, but I was a sandwich maker, not a musician. Despina are you all right?"

She was laughing so hard I had to embrace her so she wouldn't fall over. She nestled in my arms, and we both felt comfortable as little wet tears of laughter moved down her cheek.

I awoke to find Savannah Lady by my side. Once again, her beautiful head lay in her paws and she looked at me with open eyes. Only this morning, the eloquent sadness of her face displayed deep concern. Now she was seriously questioning Mother's absence.

Her butt rose, her weight fell forward onto her front legs and she let out a sharp and powerful bark that shook the room and echoed out of the house and into the morning silence.

"Savannah!" I called, lifting my head from my pillow. Again her thunderous, high pitched bark, followed by a heavy poke of her head. My ears rang and my ribs hurt.

"Savannah! For Christ's sake, what's wrong with you?"

Her head fell onto her paws, her eyelids lifted, her brown eyes asked me, "Where is Mother?"

A new day had begun and Despina was gone. "Oh, sadness,

why do you fall so heavily on me?" I asked the air. "I can barely lift myself to my feet. My heart and mind are burdened by your weight on me." I checked my watch. "Savannah! We have over-slept. John must have left for the hospital early this morning. Look, he made coffee for us," I said, as we followed the aroma into the kitchen.

We walked out to the back of the house and I poured coffee and milk into Savannah's bowl, then added pieces of hard old Italian bread. Savannah liked her coffee that way.

The green serenity of the island fairways stretched away be-fore me, a sculptured art form of earth. I heard the poetry of na-ture in a passing wind. Savannah and I walked softly, not to disturb the strange quiet of yesterday that lingered into this new day. There was again no harmony of sounds; all was silent. Birds rested on limbs stretching out from the big old trees. I felt an ab-sence, an absence of life. The energy source that fuels all things had faded, was almost gone.

We paused to sit within the stillness.

"Savannah," I asked as she sat by my side, "If my definition of love starts with the heartfelt emotion of agape, when did I em-brace love?"

Savannah sat quietly, unable to answer, but I knew she knew.

I looked up to a motionless, nonexistent sky, clear and very high. If I could look deep into the sky, would I be able to see be-yond into the heavens of another universe? I stared at the sky as my thoughts wandered into the rose garden of the night before and suddenly I remembered. It was when I looked upon her flower, deep into her eyes, the center of her bloom, that I saw into her soul and fell in love. That was the first instance of my love, the heartfelt emotion known as agape. And, as I continued to gaze upon her flower, I felt the need to touch her unique rose petals. I touched them and fell in awe, amazed by the grandeur and beauty of such softness and beauty.

Tingling vibrations traveled through my fingers and into my mind, allowing me to visualize all aspects of form through simple touch, creating a mental picture, a realization, an identity of this rose flower and of the love known as Eros.

This was the second instance of my love. Indeed, this was when I embraced love.

I stood in excitement and called out, "Oh, Savannah, I have come to know love in its entirety, love as a whole." Savannah Lady's brown eyes looked up at me with joy. I scratched the top of her head.

"You know, Savannah, I have a love for you, too. It pleases me to pet and scratch your head. Your trusting companionship and loyalty is without equal. Your love is forever giving, and I feel secure when you are by my side. You are to me like the glory of the early morning."

My thoughts reflected on this as I looked into the morning to see if I could see the glory of the early morning. And there, before my eyes, was a morning glory. It was the love in everyone's mind, a brotherhood, a companionship with all living things, a love known as Philo.

The light of the day lent a brightness and purity, and the purity gave brightness and color to all things.

Reflecting on the real and unreal, on the past and on the present, I realized the glory of companionship in the morning glory of this day.

I rose to my feet, with Savannah Lady by my side, and with a loud voice I called out, "Good morning, Despina! Good morning, God! Good morning, morning glory!" Savannah howled with me, and I vowed that from this moment on, each day when I awoke I would greet the new born day with a call. "Good morning, Despina! Good morning, God! Good morning, morning glory!"

Startled by the ring of the phone, Savannah and I hurried into the house. It was John calling from the hospital to tell us that Mother had a recurrence and was bleeding again. Dr. Higgs was rushing Mother in for an emergency operation.

Images of Despina kept appearing to me as I drove to the hospital, the visions fading and reappearing again and again.

Each time her image faded, I felt as if I were forgetting her. The feeling of being alone chilled me, so I forced my eyes to see her image on the windshield of the car. Despina's face came into focus, then slowly disappeared.

I saw Despina as she was prior to her tragedy, mature, smiling, sitting with friends, talking. Then she faded away. I saw her again as a young, spirited, liberated woman. Then once again her image faded. Another time she reappeared, and I heard her say, "George, I'm not feeling well. I think I am going to die."

Staring at my windshield feeling numb, I tried desperately to hold her image and I thought about a conversation we'd had at home one morning before leaving work.

"George," she said, "I am not feeling well these days, and I think I am going to die."

I sipped my coffee and laughed at her comment. "Don't be foolish. You're going to outlive us all. If anyone is going to pop off, it's going to be me. I am overweight and stressed out because of business. I don't eat correctly. I eat late at night and drink more than I should. So, if anyone is going to die around here, it's going to be me, not you."

Despina just looked at me, with an unusually sad and compassionate expression.

"Christ!" I called out and pounded the steering wheel, "Despina told me she was going to die. Oh, God, what have I done? Why didn't I listen to her? I could have prevented this from happening. Why didn't I take her seriously? If I had, I might have averted all this. Oh, God, what have I done?"

I kept trying to think Despina back onto the windshield, but couldn't. Why didn't I listen to her? Why didn't I take her seriously? Did I shrug her off? Was I there when she truly needed me or did I reach a point in my life where I took lovely Despina for granted, and made her feel unimportant and unnecessary?

"Despina, please Despina, don't leave me. Don't die Despina. Please don't die!"

Blood rushed to my head, and I held my breath, forcing it down inside me, thinking that this might bring Despina back into focused image upon the windshield of my vehicle. I had the feeling that as long as I kept her in my mind's eye, she would not leave me.

If she doesn't leave me, I promised, I'll make the time to listen to her attentively and take her seriously. We will sit and talk again. She will say, "George, I am not feeling well; I think I am going to die," and instead of laughing, I will embrace her and assure her that she will be well. I will fly her to Boston, to the Lahey Clinic where she will undergo tests. Her doctor will be her favorite, a Marcus Welby type. A new medication will be prescribed, and she will be well.

The light changed, I applied the brakes to stop, then said, "To hell with it," and stepped on the gas pedal. I looked out the rear view mirror. All was well. No cops. I felt the passing of that light a major accomplishment. I felt good about it.

Did Despina actually sit with me one morning and tell me she wasn't feeling well and was going to die? I struggled back into the corridors of my mind trying to return to that specific moment in time. It was, as I had just seen it, and yet it wasn't; and then it was.

A cloud of gray fell over me, obscured my vision, and lay heavily on me.

Arriving at the hospital, I jerked my car crookedly into a parking space, rushed passed the emergency sign and through the electronic doors muttering, "I hate that fuckin' sign." With thumping large steps that echoed in the empty corridor, I hurried to the elevator up to the other long white corridor and to our waiting room. How many times these past few days had I dragged my heavy feet and burdened soul through my mind into the corridors of my life? Dear God, what would I find at the end of this corridor? Will there be unknown faces, ugly and horrifying faces with evil intent? Will the flowers be bent at the stem, drooped in death?

No, I found my son and daughter radiant with love's compassion amidst a glory of color from flowers alive and well. We embraced tightly, then sat holding hands in silence. United in thought, we transmitted pleas through prayer from our cosmic consciousness to the infinite intelligence, pleading with God for Despina's well-being.

Six hours of concentrated mental thought, with words of love and then the majestic words of a common prayer flowed poetically from our lips: "Our Father, who art in heaven, hallowed be thy name."

CHAPTER 5

META ZOE

THE NURSE IN THE DISTINCTIVE starched cap entered the room. With tears from the depths of my inner soul flooding but not overflowing my eyes, I saw in a liquid haze her profile in movement.

I rubbed my eyes, irritating them, then rubbed harder as the taste of salt reached my lips. I had been wrapped in white light, an evangelistic aura of prayer, serene and heavenly, holy and divine, when I saw the nurse, also in white. Blurred, she entered the aura and for a moment I saw her as the evangel, the messenger of good news.

We gathered around to hear her words. Truly, I thought, this is an angel from God. He has answered our prayers. "Mr. Jonas," she said, "Dr. Higgs has asked me to have you wait for another hour. They are dressing Despina and wish to talk with you."

"How did everything go with the operation?" I asked.

"Dr. Higgs will explain everything," she said.

I looked deeply into her eyes, stared at her plump cheeks, and saw within her eyes compassion and fear. She moved toward D'Ann, held her hand, kissed her on the cheek and said, "Good night."

Then there was silence. We stared at one another for the longest time.

My thoughts faded. I stopped thinking. I was just a lump of

flesh and bone without thought, like an animal, conscious and receptive. How empty we can be when we can't think, when we just are.

Then D'Ann spoke, her words breaking the silence of the room. "Dad, tell us something funny."

"Something funny? I don't know, let me see, something funny." I wasn't a joke teller. What could I say, what could I find in an empty mind that would be funny? Why was it, when I was filled with words and thoughts that no one had time to listen? Now that I was naked of thought and memory, I needed words that were healing in spirit, loving, and funny.

D'Ann's childlike face pleaded, "Come on Dad, tell us something funny."

"Tell D'Ann how you and Mother met." John said "Just like you were telling me last night."

"No, that's too long, but, I'll tell you this:

"One evening, a couple of months after we had married and settled into our apartment in Woodside, Long Island, Mother thought it was time to ask Uncle Nico and his new young lady friend to dinner. So she said, 'George, please call my uncle and invite him to dinner this weekend.'

"I hesitated, then said, 'Despina, you ask him. He's your uncle.'

" 'No, George, you call him; he likes you.'

"Well, although I felt Mother should have called, I called and said, 'Uncle Nico, this is George. How are you?'

" 'Fine, my boy. My niece is a fine young lady and I am happy that you have married one another. I wish you both well,' he said in his European manner.

" 'Uncle Nico, the reason...' I started to say, but he interrupted.

" 'My brother, Nick is on his third case of Metaxa Seven Star Brandy. The first case he drank because you ran off with his daughter, and the second case he drank because he spent sixty-five thousand dollars on her education. And now I am in the process of analyzing the reason he is drinking the third case.'

"Although I was concerned, I said, 'Uncle Nico, the reason I called is to ask you to visit with us. Come to dinner this weekend.'

" 'I am indeed honored,' he replied and I felt a little better because of his enthusiastic response.

" 'Great Nico,' I said. 'How about this weekend — Saturday or Sunday?'

" 'This weekend? No, my boy, not this weekend.'

" 'Well, how about one evening during the week?'

" 'No, my boy, that won't do either.'

" 'How about a week from this coming Saturday?'

" 'No, my boy, that's too soon,' Uncle Nico said.

" 'Well, when do you think you can come?'

" 'Soon, my boy, soon. Am excited and wish dearly to visit with you and Despina.'

" 'Well then, when?'

" 'George, when I find myself and when I know who I am, I will visit with you and my lovely niece.'

" 'When you find yourself?' I repeated.

" 'Yes, my boy, when I find myself and truly know who I am, then I will visit with you.'

" 'O.K., Uncle Nico,' I said. 'I'll wait.'

" 'Kiss lovely Despina for me,' he said.

" 'O.K.,' I said and we hung up.

" 'What did he say?' Mother asked.

" 'Despina, he said he can't wait to visit with us. He is excited and honored. but, when I tried to set a date, he said it was too soon. When I asked him when he could come to dinner, he said as soon as he finds himself and knows who he is.'

"I went over to Mother, gave her a kiss and whispered into her ear, 'Despina.'

" 'Yes?' she said.

"I whispered her name, then I paused. 'Despina,' I said again as I held her in my embrace.

" 'What?' she said sadly.

"After a moment's silence, as I squeezed her to let her know that all was well and that I loved her, I whispered, 'Your Uncle Nico.'

" 'Yes,' Mother said.

"Again I paused. Then, with a loud blast of my voice, I said, 'Your Uncle Nico has gone fuckin' bananas on us! He's gonzo! Gonzo, right out of his coconut.' "

D'Ann and John broke out laughing. I smiled and wondered whether it was really funny or whether the surprise profane ending was merely shocking. The laughter soon subsided and all was quiet again as we waited for Dr. Higgs and hoped he'd come with good news about Despina's operation.

"Dad, what was Uncle Nico like?" D'Ann asked.

"How do you mean, D'Ann?"

"What did he look like?" John asked.

"Well, let me think back." I said. "I guess he was about five feet ten inches tall. He had a full head of hair swept back from his high forehead in waves, a pleasant smile, a European accent, and a way about him that women adored.

"Uncle Nico and your grandfather looked alike. They both had big noses but, more important and the reason I loved them both, they were learned men who constantly gave of their wisdom, knowledge and philosophy, although it's true that at times I thought them to be out of their minds.

"Remember now, I was only nineteen. I learned to love both these men as the years went on. They were the only fatherly influence I ever had, having come from a broken home.

"However, Mother truly needed Uncle Nico to visit with us."

"Did he ever find himself and know who he was and visit with you and Mother?" John asked.

"No, he never did, Son. That was indeed sad. Mother needed the love of family more than I, for at a very young age she was shipped off to a girl's boarding school. Nick had separated from Florence, your grandmother. Although they never divorced, I always thought their separation painfully worse than divorce."

"Why did they separate?" asked D'Ann.

"Florence left Nick to pursue her career as a concert violinist. She and Kitta, her piano accompanist moved in together and for years thereafter traveled to various countries giving concerts. Mother was without a mother from a young age, and I never knew a father. Perhaps that's why we married so young. We needed one another, and we still do."

"Did you marry Mother out of need or did you marry her because you loved her?" D'Ann asked in a serious tone of voice.

I paused. I had just been through the mental trauma of identifying my love, determining the reasons for my love, and investigating its origin. Now, under tense, desperate circumstances and a funny story comes the question of love and its humble beginnings from my daughter in an extremely sensitive frame of mind. Was it need or was it love? Perhaps both, but what of my earlier interpretation? Had I not resolved my feelings of love? "D'Ann, listen carefully to what I am about to say. Ever since this tragedy has fallen upon Mother, I have been out of my mind with the question of love.

"Dr. Higgs will be arriving soon, so I want to keep what I have to say simple. I am not going to discuss my personal feelings, for my mind has a tendency to punish me with guilt. I have felt my brain pounding and swelling against my skull these past few days for answers to why this is happening to Mother, and it has led me to question my understanding of love. I reached out to touch love but couldn't. I tried to gauge its capacity so that I could answer the question of fulfillment. Did I give enough love to Mother? What kind of love was it? Is love real and if it is, from what spring does it flow?

"Question upon question, until out of my subconscious, as if from a dream, images conveyed meaning. My grandmother came, then more mysterious images. Silently, nature revealed the creative force that gave life to a morning glory.

"Through the eyes of Savannah Lady, I understood friendship. Then I remembered from an ancient heritage the philosophy of love. I have thought of these things constantly over the past few days."

"What's the philosophy of love," John asked.

"Love is divided into three separate parts. Each is independent of the others, yet to know love the three must united.

"The first is Agape, the second Eros, and the third Philo. Each of these loves is further subdivided."

"Agape is profound and divine love, the love you have for God, the love for Mother and Father, the love first felt for a man or woman, and the love for one's children. The emotion comes from within, the psyche awakened by the pneu-ma, a breath of wind blown upon the face."

"What do you mean by Pneu-ma, Dad?"

"Psyche is the soul hidden within the depths of your mind, D'Ann. Pneu-ma is the breath of God. When He created man and woman, He blew a wind of love upon the face of his creation awakening the soul, giving it life. This is Agape."

"And Eros?" D'Ann asked.

"Eros, is the creative force within us. When the mind conceives a thought it is, in the first instance, the love of Agape. But when the thought begins to develop — the process is creative — the creative force becomes a reality, the love known as Eros.

"First, the concept translates into an emotion. Then the desire to fulfill the emotion transcends it into a physical state of being, a reality.

"For example, an artist who is driven to paint what he has seen or visualized in thought starts with inspiration, the love of Agape. Then, as the artist proceeds to paint what exists in his mind, thought becomes physical. Why? The thought transcends into a desire to perform. When the artist has completed his painting, he has experienced two fundamentals of love, Agape and Eros."

"The inspiration which is the emotion is Agape. The physical experience, Eros, is the love affair, the creative force of love.

"For the poet or the writer, the concept prefigures realization on the written page. Here, again, we experience two fundamentals of love. Now when a man falls in love with a woman, in the beginning is the emotion. After the acknowledgment of emotion comes the desire to touch, to make it physical, to know the emotion, to embrace one another passionately, to experience the sensation of the creative force — this love is Eros."

"Philo is love as friendship and companionship. A philanthropist is a friend of mankind. He gives to charity. The word derives from philo, meaning love, and anthropy, meaning mankind.

"Philo and harmony together yields love of harmony, or love of music, which is philharmonic. The city of brotherly love is Philadelphia, from Philo and adelphios, meaning brothers.

"In simple terms, the philosophy of love consists of Agape (the emotion; conception; inner thoughts and feelings), Eros (the creative force; the desire; the sensation; the will to accomplish from conception to birth or realization), and Philo (the giving of one's self to another; friendship; companionship). Now, each of these loves are independent from one another and further subdivided, creating other categories, but for our conversation tonight, we'll stay with these three fundamentals.

"To know perfect love, all three must come together as a unified whole."

"Dad, was your love for Mother complete and perfect?" D'Ann asked.

"I have questioned this deeply these past few days. Perfect love is not everlasting. It comes and goes, appears, then disappears, only to reappear again. However your understanding of love is what is important. What remains constant once you have found love is that original internal feeling. This is a flickering flame that remains lit and is manifest in respect for one another.

"So, to answer your question of how complete or perfect our love is for one another, I will say this: We respect one another; we desire one another; and we communicate well with one another."

"Yeah," said John. "But is that love?"

"Of course it is, a perfect love. By definition, respect is Agape, desire is Eros, and communication is Philo."

"But, Dad, you have expressed love in stronger terms to me," John said.

"John, judge not the height of our love from these simple

120

analogies. In moments of despair these past few days, the memories of my love with Mother are profound and divine. At this point in time I need to believe this. I don't want to accept anything less. The heartfelt feeling we have for each other is from a God-given pure heart, pure Agape."

"How is your love with Mother profound and divine?" John asked.

"Anything felt as profound and divine comes from the inner mind, from the psyche. Mother once asked me to smell some flowers she had bought. 'They're beautiful Despina,' I said, and took a quick smell.

" 'Oh, no, you don't, George. Take a deep breath and realize the true fragrance of these flowers,' she said.

"So, I took a deep breath, smelling a sweet fragrance. 'Despina, they smell as beautiful as they look,' I said. She then held my hand and together we inhaled the fragrance of the flowers. A realization came upon us as the fragrance awakened our senses. I kissed Mother. That simple experience for me was of a love profound and divine."

"Look upon your sister, John. Now D'Ann, you look upon your brother. Are you not the expression of the creative force of our love? Whenever Mother and I loved, we loved with a passion that caused the walls to sweat and the earth to tremble. And in our living from day to day over the many years, there was never a day that went by without my telling her that I loved her. We are the best of friends. True companions to one another. At times we were just lovers; at other times just good friends; but we never allowed the flickering flame of Agape to die. Respect, that deep feeling, always was present, no matter what difficulties may have been in our lives."

D'Ann and John came over to where I was sitting and embraced me, kissed me on the top of my head, as I sat with my head hung low feeling sad.

"We love you, Dad," they said sincerely.

"The problem I have not resolved is why I didn't spend more time with Mother, why I wasn't with her more often. I feel I have short-changed Mother. I never thought there would be an end to our life together. I always thought that as soon as things were just right and perfect, we would have more to give one another."

"You have given yourself in love," D'Ann said.

"Mother was right," I said. "Mother was right."

"What was Mother right about?" said John.

"In the early years of our marriage, Mother would ask me to invite my friends from school and work to our home. I would say, 'Not just yet, Despina; as soon as we upgrade our furniture I will invite them.'

"Mother would then say, 'If you are going to wait until everything is just right, then you'll never invite your friends over and that, George, would be a great loss.'

"I could have given more of myself to Mother, but I didn't. I wanted everything to be just right."

"Dad, stop punishing yourself," D'Ann called. "You were there for Mother and your family all your life. Now, stop this!" There were tears in her eyes.

"Well, I could have gone with Mother to the island beach and sat with her. She would had given me a sip of her vodka and grapefruit juice drink and we would have discussed the book she was reading. In the water, the waves would lift us together, I could have held her in such a way that when the waves set us down she would have fallen on me in a way that would have stirred passion within us."

"John, let's take Dad for a walk. Let's go for coffee. Let's get out of this room." They looked at one another with deep concern and puzzlement. "Do you think Dad's all right? He seems to be in a daze, like he's out of it." D'Ann said.

"Look D'Ann, he's trembling, like he's cold. Something is happening to him. Help me lift him to his feet."

Just then, Dr. Higgs entered. "Is everything all right?"

"My Dad's a little out of it!" John said.

"Let's get him some water."

"Coffee would be better," I said. "I'm O.K., Doctor. It's just been a long and tiring day. And John, stop telling everyone that I am out of it."

"O.K., Dad," John said.

"Dr. Higgs, I see you are still in operating garments."

"Yes," he said to me. "We have just finished dressing Despina." He waited for D'Ann to return with the coffee.

"What would we do without coffee?" I said as I sipped its warmth. I prolonged the moment for I had the feeling that I did not want to hear what Dr. Higgs was going to say. His tired face suggested failure. I had spent hour upon hour waiting to hear the results, now all of a sudden I did not want to hear anything.

"Dr. Higgs, how is my mother?" D'Ann finally asked.

Dr. Higgs looked at us, sighed, grouped us together and said, "We have lost Despina."

"What do you mean?" I asked. "Is she dead? What happened? Is she dead?"

"We found the aneurysm. It was deep within the front inner lobe of her brain. I was unable to clip it. She bled and the damage was beyond repair. We are preparing to bring Despina up now and we will put her on a life support system for a few days. I am going to ask you all to go home and get some rest. We'll talk again tomorrow. I'll be back at one o'clock in the afternoon. I'll need to speak with you all then."

John and D'Ann drifted off to a corner of the waiting room. John held D'Ann as she wept on his shoulders.

"Dr. Higgs, I'm worried about D'Ann. How will this affect her pregnancy?" I said.

"Women all over the world have suffered greater tragedies, war after war among other misfortunes, and they have given birth to healthy children time after time. Take everyone home," he said. And he left.

Through the long white corridors we slowly walked: John, D'Ann, Love, Death and I. The five of us hand in hand, walked majestically and inseparably, leaving Mother behind.

"What will happen to Mother?" D'Ann asked John.

"What do you mean?"

"I mean, will Mother go to heaven and be with God?"

"Of course," John said.

Her heavy crying was giving D'Ann hiccups and made her breathing irregular. I felt helpless sitting in the back seat of the car. John was driving and holding D'Ann's hand to comfort and console her.

"How will we know that Mother's in heaven with God? How do we know what happens after we die?" persisted D'Ann in a childlike manner. I leaned back and listened, feeling numb.

"We know Mother's with God because we will her to be with God. We see Mother with God, so she is with God. Her spirit is felt by our thoughts of her."

"What do you mean when you say her spirit is felt by thoughts of her?" D'Ann asked.

"I believe that every time I shall think of Mother, which will be always, she will be with me. She will come to me; I will see her and hear her. Her spirit will come to you and me every time we think of her," John said.

John is quite the man. All the difficulties, arguments, grievances and tense moments we have had being in business together over the past five years must have been for the good. He has the ability to reason, I said to myself as I listened to him explain things to D'Ann.

Don't be so proud, I chastised myself. Credit his mother, said my subconscious, or was it my subconscious?

"Dad, did you hear what John said?" D'Ann turned to face me.

"Is that what happens when someone dies?"

"D'Ann, I agree with John. There will soon be many questions about death, I'm afraid, and John and I will try to answer them for you as well as for ourselves."

"You know, Dad, when you talked about love, I felt something."

"Yeah, that was beautiful," John said.

"Now, tell us something about death," D'Ann said softly.

"What can I tell you about death and what happens when you die? I don't know. I have to think about it."

"You were able to tell us about love," D'Ann pressed.

"I could tell you about love because I have lived and felt love in my lifetime, but of death and what happens thereafter, D'Ann it's all new to me. I have only thought about death for a few days. but I have known love for a lifetime."

John added, "We never had to think about death before this."

"That's right, John, we haven't had to. We haven't had to because until now death's emotion has never been as strong and as real as love's emotion. We have known people who have died, some have been relatives, and though we felt sadness and compassion for their families, we've never known how the emotion can tear away at our hearts and minds."

"I want to know when I am going to feel Mother's spirit," D'Ann cried, as if she needed immediate contact to bridge love's state of mind with death's state of mind.

"In time, D'Ann, in time," I said. "Mother's spirit has not yet left Mother."

"Dr. Higgs said that we've already lost Mother, didn't he?"

"Yes, but they are keeping Mother alive mechanically. To put it crudely, Mother is half dead. Her brain is not functioning, but it still holds the psyche, the thinking mind, the soul. Her spirit will not leave her body as long as electrokinetics exist."

"What on earth is electrokinetics?" John asked.

"Electricity in motion," I replied.

"What's that got to do with Mother"

"The spirit will not leave the body as long as there is an electromagnetic field. This field of energy is generated by our hearts pumping and circulating blood throughout our body.

"When there is no blood flow or circulation because the heart has stopped, the electromagnetic field that holds the psyche, the soul, and the spirit, leaves the mind, which is the inner thought process of the brain.

"The spirit will then be released, free to roam in space, be transferred to another universe, and be recreated through love.

"Each time you think of Mother, she will hear your thoughts. It's like when you turn on your radio and receive the sound; the same happens when you turn on your thoughts. When you think of Mother her spirit will come to you. You will not be without Mother, D'Ann. None of us will be without Mother."

"But Dad, I thought you said you didn't know what happens after death."

"I don't know, D'Ann."

"Well what about what you just told us?"

"They were just off-the-cuff impressions."

We became very quiet.

The following day we met with Dr. Higgs who told us of his laborious efforts to save Despina. This time, there was deep, deep sadness and apologies for losing her. I realized that our family's love for Despina had embraced the medical staff the way the early morning mist embraces a field.

"Dr. Higgs," D'Ann said firmly, "my mother would not want to be kept half-alive mechanically."

"I understand, D'Ann," said Dr. Higgs. "Would a day or two be enough for you all to be with Despina?"

"Late this afternoon would be best," I said. "We'll spend time this afternoon with Despina, then remove her from the mechanics." We looked at one another as a strange feeling of unity — a union of empathy — encircled us. Simultaneously, we stood up. Dr. Higgs looked as if he were ready to cry. I embraced him as if I had known him all of my life and thanked him for trying so hard to save Despina.

"Dr. Higgs," a nurse called as she entered, "the room is ready now."

"You may visit with Despina now," Dr. Higgs said and led us to where she lay.

We gathered around Despina's bedside. Moments later, Fulvio and Mama arrived. Mama's prayer beads were in hand as she took her accustomed place to recite her prayers and stroke Despina's leg.

John and D'Ann took hold of their mother's hands, knowing the hand each held would not be warm much longer, that Mother herself would soon be only a memory.

Dr. Higgs left a nurse behind to attend to the medical gadgetry and to watch over Despina. I felt the need for prayer. I closed my eyes and tried to pray, but I could not. I felt betrayed; I resented our situation. Despina softened my cold heart and I spoke silently to her.

Despina, how can I now adore you? There is little room for me to come close. Even if I were to hold you in my arms, what could I say? Would I speak words of love, tell you I love you? I love you. What would these words mean the way you now are?

I have known and respected you, Despina, as a woman, as the mother of our children, as the woman who lay naked with me, and I thank you! But how will I come to adore you from this moment on? Despina, can you hear my thoughts?

Then I knew it would be with my mind. My mind was the key to all things. As long as my heart sent blood rushing through my veins, the creative force of thought within my mind will send love's emotion, Agape, and this would be transmitted to her, my everlasting love. My thought will be my adoration.

The sun's rays penetrated the window and fell on a certain corner spot on the floor. It cast the shadow of an image on the far wall. All sound muted; I was in total silence. I stepped back from Despina's bedside and walked toward the corner of the room, my eyes fixed on the beam of light. As I drew closer, my mind called out to the image, "What's the reason for all of this? Talk to me! Tell me something!" A beam of burning white light, like the ray from a magnifying glass, struck my right eye. I rubbed my eye and lost my balance. My eye felt burned. I tried to gather my senses, but I could not see out of my right eye. When I closed my left eye, everything was hazy. I could not see faces, only subdued light as if my eye were covered by a film-like substance I could not rub away. I covered my afflicted eye with my hand and with my left eye searched the wall for the image but now there was none. I looked down at the floor where the beam of light had cast the shadow, and was frightened at seeing the beam of light travel rapidly across the floor to the window and disappear.

I looked out the window and saw the sun start to set.

I was floating. Laughter was coming from the living room. Despina and her lady friends were sitting on the floor around the cocktail table sipping Chardonnay, picking on cheese and crackers, telling tales, silly talk. It happened every Wednesday afternoon.

"George, you know Helen. This is Betty, and this is Millie. Her husband owns the lumber yard."

"And whose husband is vice president of the bank?" I asked.

"That's Helen's husband," Millie said.

"Hi Helen, tell your hubby I'm coming in to hit him up for a big fat business loan." They all giggled.

"Dee was telling us stories about your experiences in Mexico," Millie said. She was a very attractive woman who looked like Ava Gardner and spoke in a southern accent.

"That's O.K., I don't mind if Despina tells you about the crazy things we did in Mexico as long as she doesn't tell you about Johannesburg," I said.

"Africa! Tell us about Africa," Helen said.

"I don't know what he's talking about. We've never been to Africa," Despina said.

"Come on George, tell us about Africa," Millie said.

"Well, before I married Despina, I was living with an African Zulu woman in Johannesburg."

"Was she black?" Helen asked as she sipped on her wine, expectations of impropriety on her plump rosy face.

"She sure was, and what a woman!"

"Don't listen to my husband. He's telling stories again; he's off in another world."

In another world, another world, echoed in my mind as I looked out the window wondering why the sun sat still on the earth's horizon.

I was brought back to our room as Dr. Higgs walked in with two women, the authoritative nurse and a doctor in surgical garments.

"Mr. Jonas."

"Yes, Dr. Higgs, we are ready," I said.

I knew he was about to ask me if we'd like a priest for prayer, and I said, "No, Dr. Higgs, we'll pray as a family together."

We gathered around Despina's bedside. Two nurses attended to the life support systems. The female doctor held Dr. Higgs' hand. We all held hands. I began to chant a Greek prayer. The language flowed although I seldom spoke it; somehow it managed to flow. I cantered like a Rabbi in his synagogue. I psalmed like a Moslem high in his mosque. And like a Greek priest, I sang the divine liturgy of St. John Chrysotom. With my good eye, I looked upon all the faces; and with my blind eye I looked inward into my mind.

As the light of day faded with the setting sun, so did the pink color fade from Despina's face. And as gray fell in its place, so did life, a perception of time, fade and end.

As my chanting echoed around the room, I saw myself as a young altar boy holding a large lit candle and following a priest, as he read from the Gospels and approached the altar, making the sign of the cross. Why did my thoughts carry me back to a time of innocence? I didn't know, but I was in the past and clearly saw a glow rise from the altar.

Clearly did I now see a glow of light rise from Despina. I fell quiet and stillness captured the moment. I stepped back from Despina's bedside after a final touch. She was cold, she had passed, the warmth had left her body, accompanied by her soul. With a last look at a glorious lady, I left.

Leaving everyone behind, I drove straight home. At home, I inserted a Tony Bennet tape, opened a bottle of Medoc and poured myself a glass of wine.

"I'll have a glass of that wine," Despina said as she entered the living room.

"Christ, I thought you would never get here. You're late — where have you been? I was worried. Come, sit." I kissed her on the cheek.

We sat in our favorite swivel chairs. A round cocktail table separated us. I reached out for her hand and smiled. "I love you, Despina," I said, and she replied, "I love you, George."

And as Tony sang, memories of the moments when our love was young danced before me.

The following day in the late afternoon, D'Ann, John and I sat at the dining room table. We were quiet, only the tinkle of red wine being poured could be heard. Everyone was solemn. D'Ann no longer looked devastated and tormented. She now had a serious, standing tall, facing-the-fact kind of look. I knew that, although her mind had shifted, her heart still bled from having been torn in two.

John's facial expressions were of deep concern. Tears were dammed behind his eyes; I suspected they ran inwardly, flooding his heart from the deep well of his soul. Oh, love, you come with so much beauty. Why does death come with so much pain?

I sat quietly observing my son and daughter, wondering what would become of us. We felt a void, an absence, as we lifted our glasses of wine and expressed our love to Mother. Good red wine, I thought, swishing around, realizing its bouquet before swallowing it. "Mr. Robinson will be here to discuss funeral arrangements," I said.

"Let's talk about that," D'Ann said.

"Fine. John, what ideas do you have?"

He paused, looked into his glass of wine and said nothing.

"How about a simple casket?" I volunteered, not knowing what else to say.

"I don't know, Dad. I just can't think about a funeral for Mother. Funeral and Mother just don't relate. I don't know; I can't imagine my mother being buried in the ground," he said.

"Especially in this low country" I agreed, "and on Hilton Head Island, below sea level. Mother will always be wet." I swallowed the rest of my wine. I wanted to retract my remark about Mother being wet. I visualized water in a crypt, a casket afloat, water seeping through and Mother being wet. What a horrifying thought! I knew both John and D'Ann saw what I pictured in my mind.

"What are you guys talking about?" D'Ann cried out. "A funeral for my mother? My beautiful mother lying in a casket. You're fuckin' crazy! I will not put my beautiful mother in a casket in a funeral home and see her dead."

"Lower your voices," I said. "Someone is coming up the walkway. It must be Mr. Robinson, the funeral director."

I went to the door, greeted him and invited him to sit with us at the dining room table where I introduced him to John and D'Ann.

"John, please pour Mr. Robinson a glass of wine."

"No, I'm fine," he said.

"Nonsense. John, pour the man a glass of wine."

"O.K., but just a small amount, please."

"Mr. Robinson, to your health," I toasted. We then drank the wine in celebration of Bacchus, the god of wine.

"You obviously have the respect of many medical professionals," I said to him. "The head nurse spoke to us about you."

"Well, thank you," he said. "I have been on the island for over twenty years."

"I appreciate your coming to our home, because I don't think we could have made it to the funeral home, either mentally or physically."

"The medical staff who cared for Despina at the hospital told me of your love and grief and asked me to visit with you. You have had a trying experience," Mr. Robinson said.

"Well, I thank you, kind sir," I said, starting to feel warm from the wine. "John! Pour the man some more wine."

"No, no more, please."

"Drink the wine, it's healthy for you. It softens the arteries while washing out the animal fats in your blood stream. "D'Ann, bring out the olives and cheese, please." The delicate-looking polite man looked at us in puzzlement. He had a slight southern accent, a round face with graying hair, and he wore a bright red sport jacket, more like a southern man making a business call than how I pictured a funeral director to look.

"These olives are from Greece," I said to him. "John, pour the man some more wine!"

"Please don't," he begged.

"Nonsense, Mr. Robinson. You're here to discuss with us the funeral and burial of our dear Despina. Do you know what I mean?"

"I th-think so," he stuttered.

"Have you always been a southern gentleman, Mr. Robinson?" I asked.

"Well, my family is from Charleston."

"Drink your wine, Robb," I urged.

D'Ann looked at John as if to say, "Boy are we in for an experience." She knew that after I've had a few glasses of wine, I become very philosophically Greek.

"Are you from Greece, Mr. Jonas?"

"No, Robb I am second generation American. My grandparents on my mother and father's side were. How do you like the cheese?"

"Interesting," Robb said.

"Good," I said. "It's made from goat's milk." His mouth opened, his chin dropped and I had to reach over and gently close it.

"Robb, enjoy your cheese, drink your wine. We have a hell of a lot to talk about." And with that he gulped.

"Dad! Don't abuse Mr. Robinson," D'Ann said.

"I'm not, D'Ann, I only want Mr. Robinson to enjoy his feta cheese. Tell me, Robb, what do you make of life after death? You're closer to it, handling the dead as you do. Have you ever wondered what's beyond?"

"Dad, Mr. Robinson is here to discuss arrangements for Mother, not to research life after death," John said.

"You're right, Son; it's a difficult subject to get into, arranging a funeral for a lost loved one, but let's start."

After a slight pause and a sip of wine, Mr. Robinson quickly said, "Mrs. Jonas is at the hospital. She has to be moved. We can arrange services for a two-day viewing. We have a lovely cemetery on Hilton Head and…"

"Jesus Christ, Robb! You certainly are quick to tell us of what has to be done."

Mr. Robinson sipped his wine and gulped like a frog. What's up with this guy, I wondered. "Hey, Robb, take off your jacket and loosen your tie."

"Well, I do have other appointments late this afternoon"

"Robb, my good man, we're talking about Despina, and we are dealing with love. Although we may be overly philosophical, we are not here to bury a dog that we loved, but a mother, a heritage, a legend. And you, my new-found friend, are not going to act like a funeral director, but as an honorable man."

Confused, Robb looked at me as I refilled my glass. He was sweating. He removed his jacket, loosened his tie, and gulped down his wine, emptying his glass. I went to his side of the table, refilled his glass with wine, put my arm around him and said, "Relax, Robb."

He looked up at me and smiled, lifted his glass, and nodded his head indicating that he understood. I acknowledged his acquiescence with a smile. "Here are pictures of our caskets with various price ranges," Robb said, taking a brochure from his briefcase.

"Dad, we have just spent thirteen days with Mother while she was in coma. To me, she was alive though she never moved or awakened. None of us want to see Mother dead. Her memory must not be destroyed by the reality of death. If we lay Mother out in a casket, in a funeral home, we will have her funeral as a final memory. But if we have just a memorial service, the image that we will reflect upon for the rest of our lives will be of our beautiful Mother alive and spirited, only dimmed by the time she was in coma in the hospital. Can we take any more than the thirteen days and nights we've just endured? I can't, and I won't. So, as far as I am concerned, there will be no caskets, no funerals, no viewing of my mother!" D'Ann said.

"What then are we to do?" I asked. "When one dies you have to have a funeral, don't you?"

"No, you don't! D'Ann is right," John interjected. "I don't want to see my mother dead, laid out in a casket. And as for you, Dad, you've just about gone bananas on us as it is. God only knows what will happen if you see Mother laid out in a funeral home."

"But, what about Mother's friends?" They will want to see Mother and pay their last respects, won't they?"

"Let Mother's friends keep the memories, of the gracious lady that she was. Let them keep the memories of her laughter and of them laughing together. Let her friends reflect upon the Wednesday night girls' gatherings, sipping on Chardonnay. Let them remember Mother's friendship. One of Mother's friends came crying to me and said, 'John, your mother was the most caring person I have ever known. I am going to miss her.' Mother was spirited and humorous to her friends. I want my mother to remain that way in the minds of her friends. I don't want them to carry away an image of her lying dead in a casket."

"You're right, John. In fact, both of you are correct. Mother was in a coma for thirteen days; that in itself has been enough. There'll be none of what they call 'viewing' for this family! Psychologically, I believe we have accepted the fact of Mother's death, have we not?" The expressions on their faces responded in the affirmative. There was no need to say anything.

"Mr. Jonas," Robb suggested, "why not consider cremation? It's not expensive."

"Robb," I said, "don't put a cost factor on our grief; money is not the issue here. It is about what are we going to do with the body of a woman who gave birth to my children and whom we deeply love. By the way, where is she now? I hope she's not in a fuckin' morgue, 'cause I'll get pissed if she is," I said heatedly.

Robb paused, then said, "As I mentioned before, she is still at the hospital."

I went over to him, put my hand on his shoulder, poured him more wine and nodded my head in appreciation of his response. Had he said, "She's in cold storage," or "at the morgue," or "in the funeral parlor," our wounds would have further deepened. These horrifying thoughts were in my mind when I asked Robb where she now was. I was most appreciative that he did not confirm my fear of Despina lying on a roll-out slab in a refrigerated box. Although inwardly, I knew it unlikely, I was happy to hear it from Robb.

"Cremation!" I shouted in a thunderous tone that wobbled the wicker lamp overhead so that its swing left darkness at one end of the table as it brought light to the other.

"What's wrong with cremation?" D'Ann asked before I could express my thoughts further. "At least my mother won't be buried in the ground. We can set her free to be with the elements — the sun, the wind, the rain. Above the earth, not beneath the earth in darkness."

I listened attentively to D'Ann, then I humbly said, "All right, I agree."

"Well, I'm not sure about cremation." John said. "Dad has our grandfather Nick in a briefcase in the closet. What will he do with Mother's ashes?"

"What!"

"Our grandfather Nick is in the closet. Dad has carried him around for years, D'Ann."

Robb trembled slightly and began eating his feta cheese and gulping down huge swallows of wine to conceal his anxiety.

"John, you're frightening your sister," I said, not wanting to embarrass Mr. Robinson by singling him out.

"Uncle Nico took his brother Nick to the island of his birth, Samos, Greece. He let the winds of the Aegean Sea carry his ashes into the heavens. And what I have in the briefcase is the small traveling bag that Uncle Nico used to carry Nick to Samos."

"Yeah, well, why are you holding onto the traveling bag?" John asked.

"When Uncle Nico returned, he asked me to keep the bag for Mother," I said.

"Why would anyone want to hold onto a bag? I'll tell you why," he said without pausing, "because Uncle Nico felt he should bring back some of his brother's ashes for Mother. Then you put the bag in an old briefcase and stuck it in the closet."

"Well, I didn't know what to do with the bag, and I didn't want to upset Mother," I said.

"Where did you put Uncle Nico? I'll bet you have him in the closet, too."

"Dad, what the hell are you doing? Starting a goddamn morgue?" D'Ann shrieked.

"State law requires—" Robb started to say, but I wasn't listening.

"No, I don't have Uncle Nico in the fuckin' closet. His wife has him with her in North Augusta. What do you think I am? A barbarian, for Christ's sake!" I shouted in annoyance.

With unsuspected courage no doubt enhanced by the wine, my new friend, Funeral Director Robinson rose to speak. The lamp was still swinging slightly and his face was alternately light and dark, light and dark.

"Mr. Jonas, cremation surely will be easier for you all. You have had enough mental punishment."

"And we will have a memorial service at the Presbyterian Church where I was married," D'Ann insisted.

John made it unanimous. "Dad, you plan the cremation with Mr. Robinson." He escorted D'Ann out of the house and they walked toward the fairway. And that was it. The decision for cremation was a relief. I had not wanted to make the decision one way or another; I could not reason whether it was the right thing to do.

"Robb," I asked as I filled our glasses, "Does this happen to other families who lose a loved one?"

"Yes, but this is the first time anyone ever got me drunk and forced me to eat feta cheese." We both laughed and drank more wine.

"What do you want me to do with Despina's ashes?"

"Robb, we'll take Despina to her favorite beach and let the sea breeze lift her to the heavens. You know, Robb, I loved her dearly. Maybe I'll keep her ashes with me. Is that normal?"

"Of course it is," Robb assured me.

"What do other people do?"

"Well, some people ask me to keep the ashes for them. Others place the ashes in a church crypt."

"Why would anyone want you to hold the ashes of a loved one?"

"Well, I guess they don't know what to do, or they cannot face up to receiving the ashes."

"Robb, do you know what love is?"

"Well, I think I do, Mr. Jonas."

"Robb, don't call me Mr. Jonas anymore. Call me George, O.K?"

"O.K., George."

"To your health, Robb." A musical note rang from the clinking of our glasses. "Where were we? Oh, I know, I asked you about love."

"Yes," said Robb.

"Picture this Robb: you walk into a garden full of roses." I was having trouble articulating, the effect of too much wine. "And in this garden among all these beautiful roses, your eye sees one rose in particular. You approach the rose; you look at it for a moment. You lean over to breathe in its fragrance, then you touch the rose, feel its softness, realize its form, its beauty. You pluck it from its stem, take it home, place it in water, live with it until it fades and dies. That is love and I guess, that is life too. At any rate, that is where I am now. What do you think, Robb?"

"Well, you certainly summed up life and love pretty well, I think." Then he fell quiet.

"Robb, are you O.K?"

"I'm a little bit tired. I should be getting home. I've been here too long."

"But look at the philosophical experience you've had," I exclaimed. "Are you going to handle the memorial service and cremation in a manner befitting my lovely Despina, Robb?"

"Of course, George! There is no other way, I promise."

"Robb, there is one more thing."

"What's that?"

"I want you to deliver Despina's ashes to me personally. I also want you to promise me, and I will put this in writing, that when I die you will cremate me and mix my ashes with Despina's. Mix them together so that we become one in ash, one united in soul; then take us to the Palmetto Dunes Plantation. At the Arthur Hills Golf Course on the fifth green by the waterway, about thirty yards from the green, is a wooded area. It's a very beautiful spot, you can't miss it. One day, I'll show you exactly where it is. The spot sits high on the embankment. There is always a breeze passing through the beautiful trees and bushes. There, on that spot, I would like you to place our ashes. Then as the wind whistles through, it will lift us with the morning glory and carry us up into the heavens. Will you do this for me?"

"Of course," Robb said with tears in his eyes.

D'Ann and John were back and astonished to find me and Robb in our cups.

"Dad, Mr. Robinson has to go home," D'Ann said. "It's late and it's dark out, and you've gotten the poor man drunk."

"O.K."

"I'm fine," Robb said, tightening his tie.

"John and I are going to Fulvio's restaurant. We will drive you home."

"No need for that."

"Oh, yes there is, Mr. Robinson," John said. "We need you for Mother's memorial service, and you won't be there for us if you're in the clinker."

"Clinker?"

"The jail house, Mr. Robinson."

"Dad, how much wine did you and Mr. Robinson drink while

John and I were gone? Christ, all of Hilton Head Island is going to know that you got Mr. Robinson drunk. I'm humiliated and embarrassed."

"Don't let it bother you, D'Ann. You have enough to think about. Now take Mr. Robinson home."

John helped Robb to his feet. The funeral director waddled into John's arms, and was steered out the door and into the car. I watched and waved as they backed out of the driveway. The dark of night had covered the island. Everywhere I looked was very dark, pure black.

Now I really felt alone. Everyone was gone. Even Savannah Lady was at a dog motel. Despina's gone! I walked through the empty rooms, just looking and walking and looking. What was I searching for? On the dining room table sat four empty bottles of Medoc wine. I dimmed the dining room light and looked outside. Flood lights pointed up the trunks of several old trees, creating a strange beauty. However, I could not penetrate the loveliness; the wine was like a mist between my sight and my mind.

I followed the row of plants along the glass wall of the house. I touched their person, felt their pulse beat, caressed and held their leaves. I asked the beautiful plants how long they would live. "How long is your life?" I said out loud. The plants smiled at me, assuring me that they would not leave me. Before my eyes, a bud flowered and the bloom whispered to me, "I love you."

Pleased that I was not alone, I fell on the sofa and was instantly asleep.

CHAPTER 6

OF EQUITY AND GOOD CONSCIENCE

THE MEMORIAL SERVICE was elegant and dignified. Mr. Robinson handled every detail perfectly and beautifully.

Thereafter, I applied myself diligently to the family business. I kept myself busy, but never before had I experienced such low spirits. At night, loneliness and a bottle of wine were my companions.

I sought to find relief with Savannah Lady, as a man in need might turn to his dog for companionship. Savannah Lady was worse off than I, however lethargic and melancholy. Her beautiful head hung low. I felt bad for Savannah, knowing her need for Despina's love and companionship. To some extent, I could soothe my feelings with wine, embracing forgetfulness and then sleep. I could scream, cry, kick and swear, express myself. Savannah could not.

I was amazed by her sensitivity, her awareness of Despina's absence and the deep sorrow that removed her spirit from her soul.

There may be degrees of consciousness and intellect, the different abilities that separate man and dog, but both know the same sorrow and depression when a loved one is no longer present.

When I was able to express myself enthusiastically to Savannah, I noticed, she would feel better and I would feel better.

When my enthusiasm waned, our uplifted feelings would diminish.

Enthusiasm, what does it really mean? One day, out of curiosity I looked it up in Webster's. I thought I knew its meaning, but found I did not. I had assumed I understood the word, but the dictionary revealed its true and complex meaning along with its etymology: To be inspired, be possessed by God, full of God, having God within; inspiration; from the Greek *enthusiamus.*" Savannah lifted her head and barked as I read aloud its meaning to her.

A sense of security comforted me for the moment, for I had found one of life's secrets in the definition of enthusiasm: to be inspired. "Having God within."

I could be inspired. I could be enthusiastic. And certainly I could find God within, or could I? Despina's death had removed meaning from my life; would enthusiasm, true enthusiasm, give me new feeling and meaning? Would I now find a purpose for my existence and no longer be without reason for being.

How could I be inspired? How could I find God within so I might live on?

That summer, intense heat that reached the high nineties visited Hilton Head almost daily.

The heat made me wish I were back in New England, but the demand for ice cream soared. Our small company, Masterbrand Distributors, moved five trucks daily throughout South Carolina, servicing major supermarket chains, convenience stores and restaurants.

D'Ann was now working with Fulvio at his restaurant. John traveled throughout the state servicing accounts and I ran the office. Our years of development, investment and devotion to the ideals of business success in the American tradition of hard work and sweat equity were threatened by the deceptive game plan of Popular Foods and the Famous Ice Cream Company.

"George, John is on the phone," Emily called out. "He needs to talk to you. It's important!" I picked up the phone.

"Dad, I just left Main Super Market in Columbia. Ralph, the frozen food manager, told me that Famous Ice Cream is establishing an office in Charlotte, North Carolina. Ralph told me that within six months, all super markets would be serviced directly by Famous Ice Cream, and they're going to give out money allowances and promotional benefits."

"John, what are you saying?"

"Dad, Famous Ice Cream has made a deal with super markets. They are going to put the screws to us."

"They don't have to steal our customer accounts. Famous Ice Cream makes the finest, purest ice cream in the world."

"Dad, we're not talking about the quality of the product. We're talking about business ethics, principles and morality."

"Don't forget, John, Peterson said he would have our agreement to us in a couple of months."

"Dad, Peterson has been promising you that agreement for four and a half years. He lied to us when he came down to see us when Mother was in the hospital."

"John, I have never heard you sound so concerned."

"Dad, they put a gun to Jerry's head to force him to sell them his Atlanta distribution. Remember how Jerry told us they were going to walk in and take our business? You better find out what South Carolina law says about equity and good conscience," John emphasized.

"I am going to call Famous Ice Cream and ask them about

what Ralph told you. Then I'll call McPherson. Don't worry, John; no one is going to steal or take anything from us that we paid for and built up. No one can take our distribution channels away from us. They have to buy what we created with the sweat of our brows."

"Dad, don't be naive. Listen to me: Famous Ice Cream and Popular Foods are starting to put the screws to us. I see little things happening that trouble me. They planted a representative in Charlotte, North Carolina. Now rumor has it that they are going to take over our accounts in South Carolina and Georgia. Instead of Famous Ice Cream helping us promote their products, they are causing chaos. I'll tell you more this weekend when I return to Hilton Head."

The conversation troubled me long after we hung up. I felt stripped naked and thrown into the street. To lose our investment and five years of our lives would destroy us as a family. We wouldn't be able to repay our loans and if our business failed many other families would suffer.

I sat back in my chair, put my feet on the corner of my desk, closed my eyes and allowed my thoughts to wander. "Despina, where are you? I need you near me. I miss you and I think I would like to die."

"George," Emily called out as she entered my office, "here's some coffee." In a determined tone she added, "I've worked with you for some time now, and if anyone can handle the Popular Foods Company, you can."

"Emily, you heard my conversation with John?"

"Yes, I did. John is correct. Famous Ice Cream has caused us great difficulty these past weeks, disrupting our office with calls for a list of our accounts and other matters of information that were of no concern to them."

"Emily, close my door. I am going to call Peterson." She left me with a cup of hot coffee and an expression of deep concern and personal pain. An image of her African American and American Indian heritage flashed in my mind. I saw her forebears crying, standing alone, while smoke rose, flames whipped, and men in blue uniforms rode off. I had a new thought. If Famous Ice Cream wouldn't buy our business, if they tried to take it, wouldn't the law consider that grand theft? I wondered what a lawyer would call it?

But if they did not want us as distributors, why did they authorize us to become their distributors and give us a letter of appointment? Why have us invest in capital equipment and promote and sell their products for five years? Why allow us to build a Famous Ice Cream distribution network in South Carolina? Why was I imagining the worst, affirming a destructive image in my mind? Why would they want to put us out of business? I decided to become enthusiastic, inspired. I decided to talk to God. With my hands together, my eyes closed, my head down, I whispered, so Emily would not hear me, "Dear Father in heaven above, I am truly troubled. Despina is no longer. Our small company and its employees are afraid. They sense that something sinister is happening. Guide me, if you will. Please!"

Moments passed. I gazed out the office window at pink- and rose-colored flowers of the hibiscus. Feeling slightly inspired at having talked to God, believing that my call to him had been heard, my eyes remained fixed on the reflected colors from the flower and saw Despina. Her green eyes communicated with me. What was she trying to tell me? I tried to picture it but could not. I knew however that a thought or something had been sent. Despina faded away and a new face came forward, angelic, with green eyes and golden hair. After the briefest moment, it too faded.

I turned from the window, sipped my coffee, then for some reason ran like a madman outside the office and around to the back of the building. I searched the hibiscus bush for the face I had envisioned. I thought I was going crazy. Should I pluck the flower, or leave it as it is? If I took the flower, plucked it from its stem, I could look at it in my office until it died. However, if I left the flower, I could admire it through my window. If I plucked it, it would die in a short time. If I left it on the bush, it might live longer and I wouldn't be responsible for its premature death.

Everything dies, I thought; when will I die. Might it be when the flower fades on the bush? Sadness engulfed me as I slowly walked back to the office, dragging my whole being. Why was I, from minute to minute, in a different state of mind? Oh, God, how much can my heart and mind take?

Emily was standing on the deck leading to our office. "There is someone here to see you."

"Who's that?"

"Mr. Patrick from the Hilton Business Brokerage. He's been calling you for days."

I greeted him with a handshake, and offered him coffee. "Let's go into my office. What can I do for you, Mr. Patrick?" I asked as he seated himself.

"Call me Pat."

"Fine, and you may call me George."

"About five months ago, George, you talked with a Mr. Singleton about selling your business. Mr. Singleton is no longer with our firm, and I am following up on all his contacts. I have his file on Masterbrand Distributors, and I would like to review his notes with you. Are you interested in selling your company?"

"Well, I almost forgot about Mr. Singleton. "He was to get back to me with responses from interested parties."

"Well, I believe one of those interested groups would like to talk with you further."

"Where are you from?"

"Ohio. And where are you from?"

"Boston, originally, but I came to Hilton Head from Virginia. Tell me, Pat, what brought you to Hilton Head?"

"I became enchanted with the beauty of the island plantations."

"The beauty of the island plantations," I repeated as he searched through his briefcase for our file. His somewhat youthful face was scarred by life. He had blonde hair, blue eyes, and a Southern manner, typical of many islanders, but he was extremely thin and pale, almost white, while most locals were deeply tanned by the hot island sun. "How long have you been on the island, Pat?"

"Just over five years."

"Me, too. Do you have a family?"

"Sure do, three children."

"That's great. A big happy family." I pictured a complete family with a woman alive and well, thinking of Despina and my family.

With a tremble in his voice, hesitating, he stuttered, "That's about to end."

"What's about to end?"

"My wife is going to leave me. We're filing for divorce."

"I'm truly sorry to hear that, Pat."

"I've resigned myself to it. This whole island is full of broken homes."

I felt badly for him, just as I felt badly for myself, associating his loss of a wife, although not quite the same, with my loss of Despina.

"What about you, George. Are you married?" Pat said.

"Not any more. Despina passed away."

"I am sorry. Your wife's name was Despina?"

"Yes. Tell me, Pat," I asked, taking a deep breath hoping to relieve the depression I felt coming on, "what did Mr. Singleton have in his notes about our distribution network. And what about this group that may want to buy us out? "

"Before we get into that, George, let us pray together." He leaned forward in his chair, resting his supplicating hands on my desk.

"Pray together?" I felt awkward, somewhat embarrassed, somewhat put off by the liberties he was about to take. Not knowing how to handle the situation, I said, "I don't know if I want to pray to God. I am pissed at God." Pat sat up, dismayed, a hint of compassion on his face. "Besides, praying to God is a personal matter," I added.

"When was the last time you prayed?" he asked.

"Just before you arrived I talked to God. In fact, I've been talking with God ever since Despina died. Maybe it wasn't God I was talking to; maybe I was just talking to myself. I have been a little crazy these days, but even if I prayed and talked with God that doesn't mean he is one of my favorite people these days."

"You need to pray to God humbly, not talk to God. You need to find Christ, George!"

"I found Christ long ago, Pat. I am beyond Christ and into another dimension of belief and thought. I am one with the universe, one with infinite intelligence."

"Sometimes, George, we need to get back to the basics, to take a step backwards in order to move ahead spiritually and into an advanced dimension of thought and belief. At present, I can tell you that you are totally without God and the universe."

"I haven't known you more than thirty minutes," I said. "I don't know whether to throw you out on your ass or consider you as one who has come into my life for good reason."

"Please, George, let us pray together."

His plea was so sincere that out of respect for his belief, I submitted. With his eyes closed and his hands folded, he leaned forward and the words flowed from his mind as he prayed for Despina, my family, his family, the business relationship we were to enter into and for me to come to Christ. He prayed that Christ would walk with me and inspire me into levels of meditative thought so that I might be as I wished.

Pat's plea for me to visualize Christ as the source for conceptualization, to tap the inner source of my mind, was new to me. Christ belonged to obsolete religions that had driven young people to Eastern philosophies and cultures. I had set Christ aside many years ago, thinking that belief in Christ was passé. I needed to develop my inner intellect, my subconscious and cosmically conscious mind, my self knowledge in other dimensions of thought. All my prior relationships with religious doctrine and concomitant social rules had been abandoned, fallen from grace.

Pat's prayer ended. He smiled as he returned to the real world, but I still felt the intense pure energy of his prayer. He had truly prayed for my well-being, not with quotes or clichés for my salvation, but with words created from the depths of his inner thought process. I felt good, for I had experienced a realization. Pat felt good, for he had an evangelistic experience.

I looked out the window in search of a woman's image in the bloom of the purple and rose-colored flower, but, she was not there. "I am confused, Pat," I said as I turned from the window. "How can you, a man with words of divine love in prayer, pure faith and fellowship, be without reason?"

Silence filled the room. "What do you mean?" he asked.

"I appreciate your words of prayer and your kind of thoughts. Although, at first, I resented your effort. I learned something from your prayer."

"What was that?"

"As I listened to your prayer, visualizations appeared in my mind. From now on, when I meditate, I will form an image of Christ in my mind and I will walk with him into a new field of thought. There I shall find enlightenment, tranquillity and order to my mind. I will be one with God and the universe. The problem I have this moment is with you. How can you be in such fellowship with me, A man you've just met, yet not be in fellowship and in love with your wife who gave birth to your children? Is the profound beauty of your prayers for others an over abundant energy of divine love that takes energy away from your wife and family? Are you giving it all to your church and fellowship, then returning home exhausted and without any love left for your family? If you are, then you will fail in your evangelistic mission, for to deny your wife love's emotion, love's companionship, love's touch and expression, is not what your God wants of you."

Pat's head fell and remained bowed as he said, "You're right. I have denied my beautiful wife love and companionship while I pursued glory and fellowship for the church. I am ashamed."

"Don't be ashamed. Go home and tell your wife you love her. When was the last time you told her that?"

"It's been a long time."

"Pat, look at me! Don't you see written on my face pain and torment from the loss of a loved one? Is there not loneliness and desperation for companionship? Come here, look out this window. Do you see that bush with the rose-purple flower?"

"Yes, I see it."

"I look at it every chance I get. I think I see Despina's face in it, but then it fades and I see another woman's face. I have an excuse for my insanity: my wife died. You have no excuse for your insanity: you still have your wife. In fact, you have it all. Go home and when you enter your house, smile. Bring your wife a simple flower. Approach her with warmth and friendship. Kiss her on the cheek and whisper into her ear that you love her. Tonight, when you are both in bed, hold her tightly. Make her feel secure. Let her lie in your arms. Allow her to speak, let her tell you of her day and listen attentively to what she says. Give her what you gave to me and what you walk about town giving to others: simple friendship.

Each morning when you walk out of the house, call in a loud voice, 'Good morning, Mary. Good morning, God. Good morning, Morning Glory.' Stop and look around you. Appreciate the beauty of the day in its morning glory."

"George, that was beautiful. You should write down what you just told me."

"I have, Pat; I have. The only outlets I have had to help me while I grieve have been a bottle of wine, my dog, and writing down my simple thoughts."

"May I read them?"

"They are very personal. Perhaps one day." We agreed to let business matters rest until the following morning and shortly thereafter Pat left and Emily looked in.

"What was that all about?"

"Miss Emily," I replied in a soft southern voice, "that there was all about life."

I knew she had heard parts of our conversation for the walls of our office were thin.

"I thought you had different views on religion," Emily said.

"I do. We weren't talking about religion."

"Then what's happening with Mr. Patrick's wife?"

"Now Emily, we won't have any of that nonsense."

"Well, I know you've been busy and troubled and I haven't had time to discuss business with you, but our new part time girl starts work next Monday."

"Thanks for briefing me."

Emily raised an eyebrow, then turned and limped toward her computer. When her mind and body were weary, she sometimes walked off balance. I ran after her and whispered, "I'm sorry, Emily. I know I haven't been much help to you these past months. Forgive me." She rewarded me with a smile.

The following morning Patrick arrived with new enthusiasm. We had coffee in my office, and this time he did not insist on prayer. I was pleased. "Before we talk business," he said, "I want to let you know what you have done for me, my wife and my family."

"Done for you and your family? What have I done for you?"

"During the hour and a half drive home yesterday, I reflected on our meeting and conversation. By the time I reached home, I had fixed in my mind exactly how I was going to approach Mary and what I was going to say to her. I started out in a clumsy manner by asking her to sit for I had something to tell her. She hesitated and trembled slightly but did as I asked. Then, well, then," he stammered.

"Then what?" I urged. "Get on with it."

Exhaling, red-faced, he said, "I fell to my knees and begged her to forgive me. 'Forgive me, Mary for denying you my love. It has made us disrespect and disregard one another.' Then I told her that I truly loved her."

"What happened then?"

"She cried. She took my head on her lap and with her trembling hands she caressed me and said that she loved me, too, with all of her heart but that she needed to know and be loved by me. We talked, away from the children, until three o'clock in the morning. I did what you said."

"And?"

"I held her tightly and assured her of my love. I pressed my naked body against hers, inhaled the fragrance from her hair and repeated the words, 'I love you, Mary.' "

"That was beautiful. I am proud of you."

"You have saved me from making a terrible error, from destroying my marriage, my home, my life. In less than twenty-four hours, I have changed the course of my life merely by redirecting some of my energy, love's energy, towards my home."

"Pat, to hold Despina in my arms one more time so that I might realize the wonder of love's embrace would mean everything to me. It would truly be a glorious moment."

I looked out the window to gaze on the flower of the hibiscus bush, but it was no longer there. I leaned against the window to see if the flower had fallen to the ground, but I could not see it.

"Pat, please excuse me for a moment. Help yourself to another cup of coffee. I'll be right back." I ran out of my office.

"You're not leaving, are you George?" Emily asked.

"No, I'll be right back. I am only going around to the back of the building."

Emily's eyes rolled but there was a smile on her face as I rushed past her.

I hurried around the building to the hibiscus bush but could find no flower, just scattered leaves and petal fragments.

"Christ, I even lost the flower! Oh, God, how much more do you want from me? You have left me so empty, so empty and alone," I cried. Looking up, I noticed Pat standing, looking out at me from my office window. I waved and smiled as if everything was normal, though I felt a deep loss. To cover up, I looked around as if searching for something I'd dropped. I bent down, snatched at a petal, put it in my pocket and glanced back up. Emily was standing alongside Pat, and she fixed me with her piercing brown eyes. I smiled, patted my pocket, then walked back to my office, whistling and pretending to be in control but thinking, "I won't be able to look on the flower and see Despina; I won't be able to identify the other image I had seen in the flower, even if I'd only seen it for a microsecond.

Pat had rediscovered love with Mary, found what I had lost. Was I happy for him? I have lost Despina, the flower, the image of an unknown woman: Agape, Eros, and Philo. My heart was empty of love's emotion. I longed for love's companionship. Emptiness echoed within my heart and mind filling me with its pain and torment. If something can be felt from nothing isn't that an emotion? When nothing is felt from something, isn't that non-existence emptiness? The loss of a flower, giving thought to my mind; the loss of Despina, giving love to my heart.

"Did you find what you were looking for?" Emily asked.

"No, Emily, I did not. It was carried off with the wind. Perhaps tomorrow, when the wind returns, I'll find what I am looking for."

Emily's eyes not only rolled but looked up as if in prayer, begging the Lord to return my sanity to me.

"Pat, pardon the interruption," I said as I positioned myself in my office chair. "Now, what's up with the potential buyer for our distribution company?"

"George, will you visit with me and Mary some day this week? We need you to talk with us, possibly to share your thoughts on love with us. Our church members call upon other church members in their homes every Thursday night. Your thoughts and words would be welcomed."

"Pat, I am neither a marriage counselor, an expert on love, nor an evangelist. I am just simply a man who has lost his wife and companion to death. I want her back, and I can't have her. Therefore, when you tell me that you are about to leave your home, your wife and your family, I tell you that you are a fool and not deserving of a woman. I advise her to run away from you, to fall on my doorstep. I will take her in, embrace her and she will come to love me. For now, I am without, and because I am without I have become a learned man of love. I know how to love, respect and adore a woman."

"But, that's what I mean," Pat said. "I need to know that, too."

"Pat, when death comes to take your wife, you too will learn of love. But if you are asking me to discuss the pain and torment in my heart and mind arising from my grieving, then you are asking a lot of me and I wonder about your compassion."

"George, I am not without compassion. Mary and I just want to hear your sensitive words. They mellowed me and taught me something about my relationship. I have never heard anyone speak about love, with such tenderness, and I'll admit to the world it has made me rethink the course of my life."

"I didn't mean to be hard on you, Pat but you must understand what I am going through."

"Despina must have been some kind of woman."

"She was like all women. The only difference was that we were in love. My friend Robert said it best at the memorial services when he said, 'Despina was a strong woman who owned and loved her life and shared it willingly with others.' I remember her saying, 'George, let's go to Quaker services this Sunday. It's held in a beautiful setting, with tall trees and lovely flowers. We'll sit quietly with Mother Nature.'

"Did you go?"

"No, I didn't."

"Why not?"

" 'Cause I was a stubborn bastard. I now realize that loving was not enough. Time, quiet time together, is necessary for the companionship of love. It rained last night, didn't it?"

"Yes, it did."

"I was alone last night and drank a half bottle of wine, about two glasses, then put on one of my favorite operas, La Boheme. I wandered through the rooms wondering, thinking, reliving scenes with Despina, talking to plants, just being very much alone.

"Lightning, the rays of God, snapped in anger at the earth; then the rain fell. It fell hard, beating down on the trees, bushes and flowers. The sound of the falling rain intrigued me, for it beat in time to the music from the stereo.

"I walked out of the house to where its light met the black of night. I heard Despina call, 'George, I am here with you.' I listened as rainwater soaked me. I took off my shirt so my body could feel and absorb the tears from the heavens. I called out, 'Despina, I am lost without you. You left without my love's embrace, without a tender kiss from your lips.'

"She spoke to me through the sounds of rainwater, assuring me of her love. 'The flowers will blossom with my love for you; look deep into their bloom; breathe in their fragrance; feel their softness.' The pores of my body opened, and rainwater flowed into my bloodstream and carried love into my empty heart. Chilled by a passing wind, I went back into the house and was about to enter when I noticed a limb of a hibiscus bush broken by the heavy rain. It bore three deep red flowers. I plucked the flowers from their broken stem and brought them into the house. Pouring myself a glass of wine, I sat at the dining room table and gazed at a flower for a long time. Transparent pearls of rainwater on the petals slowly moved to the flower's heart where they formed a small pool of water. I saw myself reflected in the pool. I looked tired. I had aged.

"Then I heard Despina say, 'George, spread the petals of the flower. Drink the rainwater from the flower's heart. It will give you youth and virility so that you may find another woman's love, a love such as we have known. Place your lips on the bloom. There within and just above your lips will embrace the stem within the flower's bloom. Now love me a final time.' "

"George, your heart is not an empty heart. It's a heart full of love. All you need is to find another woman to love."

"Pat, I could never love another woman."

"Of course you could."

"I don't think so. Besides, what woman today would have a madman like me? It would have been easier for me to love another woman when Despina was alive — for I knew she was there — at home — constant, remaining as unchanged in love as a century-old tree has stood stalwart. It would have been easier to know another when Despina was alive, but I now feel I must respect her memory and my adoration."

Pat started to respond, but I was listening to fainter sounds. All I could think of were words that troubled me: "Now love me a final time Now love me, a final time."

Pat kept appearing and fading from my vision. I was floating, distant, elsewhere. Something like a spirit was leaving me, or a magnet pulling at something within me.

"Despina, what did you mean by love me a final time? Despina, are you leaving my heart and mind? Are you withdrawing from the inner me, leaving me with an empty, empty heart, a heart without your love, a mind without the memory of your love?"

Despina responded, "Last night your heart was flushed with a new and vibrant love from the rainwater that fell from the heavens. This pure fluid of Agape will energize your mind, your psyche, and be a new inspiration for you. In time a new love will come to you."

"George, will you do it? Will you do it?" Pat was asking.

"Do what?" I asked, as my feet touched the ground. Pat emerged from a haze and entered my vision.

"Come to my home?"

"Yeah, O.K." Dazed, I began traveling at the speed of light. I was trying to be responsive to Pat, yet I couldn't help thinking about last night's experience and my having told Pat of my personal ordeal. Despina's "love me a final time" meant she had withdrawn her love from my heart and mind. Although death had inspired a love within me I had never felt before, never known to such a degree of expression or realization, I, now Meta-Zoe, after life, was experiencing the withdrawal of love's emotion. A new loss, a new emptiness, a new non-existence rose within me. How could I abandon what was left of a familiar love?

My office door opened abruptly, and Emily entered with fresh coffee, which was her way of telling me to stop the nonsense and get down to business. "Pat, let's talk about the sale of this distributorship," I said, winking at Ms. Emily for her kind offering and timely interruption.

"There are interested parties who want to talk to you," Pat said. "However, we need to establish a few things. When Mr. Singleton called the Famous Ice Cream Company to verify that you were the appointed distributor, they said that you were and had been for five years. But when one of our clients called Famous Ice Cream to confirm the report, he was told that you owned nothing."

"What?!" I shouted.

"Wait," Pat said. "Mr. George Strathmore of the Hilton Head Bank and Trust also called to confirm your rights to distribute Famous Ice Cream in South Carolina, and he was told that you were the distributors, having purchased the distributorship with their approval back in 1983. Mr. Strathmore told Mr. Singleton that he had approved a $110,000 loan to Masterbrand Distributors based on his conversations with a vice-president from Famous Ice Cream. Why is Famous Ice Cream now taking the position that you own nothing?"

"Pat, I bought this business when it was doing less than sixty thousand dollars a year. It's now touching the one million mark annually. John and I poured big bucks into capital equipment and five years of sweat equity into the development of our franchise. Believe me, we own what I purchased, which was the right to distribute Famous Ice Cream. We have a letter of appointment, a bill of sale, and a general warranty. I own what I purchased and paid for, and I have the right to sell my business to any approved investor.

"You know, Pat, it may not be the Famous Ice Cream Company that's behind the deception. It may be the Popular Foods Company."

"Well one of the interested buyers owns a milk distribution company in New Jersey. Famous Ice Cream wouldn't have a problem approving the sale of the Masterbrand Distributors to them," Pat said.

"When John and I bought this business we knew nothing

about ice cream other than selling Chipwich on the beach. We were successful with Chipwich sales, so we decided to expand our business with another quality product. We had no prior frozen food experience, no trucks, no freezers. If we were approved to purchase the distribution without any experience, a milk company out of New Jersey shouldn't have a problem receiving Famous Ice Cream approval. Set the appointment, and I'll talk with them. In the meantime, I'll straighten out what I own and don't own with Famous Ice Cream."

"I am sure we can get things right," Pat said. "I'll call the New Jersey people. I also know three other groups that have a sincere interest."

"Fine," I said.

"Don't forget now, you said you would visit our home."

"All right, one day next week," I said before Pat left.

"Emily," I called. "Will you be kind enough to get our attorney on the phone while I search for some papers that I must talk to him about."

Shortly thereafter, I met with Mr. McPherson at his office. He was not surprised when I informed him of Patrick's findings.

"George, when you told me of Jerry's experience with Popular Foods Company when we met with Peterson, I called Jerry in Atlanta. He confirmed everything you had said about Popular Foods putting a gun to his head. Earlier this week I received his sworn deposition. I'll make you a copy."

While he was making the copy, I thought of the reports Pat had read and of John's words as they replayed in my mind. I reflected on my meeting with Famous Ice Cream and of the unethical, obscene behavior of Popular Foods. My heart was heavy.

"Here is your copy," Mr. McPherson said as he handed me a sheaf of papers.

"Oh God!" I cried out as I drove from his office. "How much more weight must I carry within my heart and mind?"

I had to find relief. I'll check in with Emily, then I'll leave, I thought, but I encountered a new face when I arrived at the office. "George, this is Karen," Emily said, "She's our new part-time person. Karen says you know her husband."

"I do?" Puzzled, I looked at Karen's face.

"Rick speaks highly of you," Karen said.

"He does? How do I know him?"

"He's your barber. He cuts your hair."

"Rick the barber is your husband? Well, you tell him he's one lucky guy to have such a pretty lady. Welcome to our office, Karen." I retreated into my office, closing the door behind me.

I went to the window to look at the hibiscus bush. It had changed. The leaves were larger and a darker green.

Pacing the floor I picked up the phone and called Peterson at Famous Ice Cream. "Mr. Peterson, I am holding a sworn deposition from Jerry in Atlanta. He testifies under oath that a Vice-President from Popular Foods in Chicago said to him, and I quote, 'Jerry, we're not putting a gun to your head, but if you don't sell your distribution to us, we're going to put our trucks in Atlanta and put you out of business.' His deposition goes on to say that Famous Ice Cream was going to come in and take my business, my distribution."

"George, I can't believe that!"

"Mr. Peterson, I am holding a sworn affidavit."

"George, your distribution agreement should be in your hands in sixty days. I'll send you a letter to that effect. Trust me, no one is going to take your business from you and John."

"Mr. Peterson, I don't know what to believe. I'm putting my trust in you. I'll wait for your confirming letter."

I sat with my elbows on my desk and rested my heavy head in my hands, my palms pressing against my eye sockets. The pressure on my eyes comforted me. I watched white lights flash across my mind until, suddenly, as if on a movie screen, I saw myself dancing in the rain. In the swiftly falling rain, high in the sky, I was dancing on top of the pyramid of Teotihuacan in Mexico. Had I called out to God then, asking for his favor, when I was so close to the heavens? Had I failed him somehow? Was this why I was being stripped of love's harmony? Was this why I was without love and its spirit of life? I saw it clearly. A long time ago I did dance on top of a pyramid in a maddening rain. I remembered everyone running down the pyramid, down slippery stone steps as I called out to my family and to others.

"Where are you running to? The rain is coming down there as well as up here. It's everywhere. You might as well stay up here with me." Then, in celebration of my madness, I danced. I danced the way a Greek man dances: by himself, for himself. Then I danced to please the gods. I danced to honor the heroes of the past. I danced to life and to love. After a joyous time, drunk with being, I became a translucent pearl of rainwater and slid down the pyramid.

In my path an Indian woman with a vinyl poncho covering her head hurried toward me.

"Maia, Maia," she called. "Maia, Maia." She held out a flute made of clay. It was about eight inches long, and in front of the lip section was a face from the stone calendar. I reached into my pocket for money when a young Indian boy appeared, dripping wet.

"The woman does not want any money. It is a gift for you," the boy said, then translated, "The old woman asks you if you were born in the month of May."

"Yes," I said, "but, why does she ask?"

The Indian boy spoke to the old woman and then said to me, "She said she has waited many years for a man born in the month of May to dance on top of the Pyramid of the Sun."

"Is that what the pyramid is called, the Pyramid of the Sun?"

The boy assured me it was.

"And what is this face on the flute?"

The boy spoke to the old woman again. "She says it is the face of Ahau of the Maya."

I looked at the flute. The face was square with rounded corners. It had two small, penetrating eyes, with a long double line for a nose, and a round mouth. I blew a screeching musical note, then asked, "What does it mean?"

The boy said, "The old woman says that in thirteen years a light as bright as the sun will come to you, and you will begin to know." Then the boy and the old Indian woman walked away.

I looked at the flute, then put it in my pocket. In thirteen years the light would come to me. I stood in awe and in the rain. "Hey, wait!" I called and ran over to join the boy and the Indian woman. "Young man, where is this woman from?"

"She is from the Sierras of Chiapas."

"Where's that?"

"Near Guatemala."

"Guatemala! That's another country! Is she Mexican?"

"No, she is Mayan."

"Oh." I said. I went closer to the Indian woman. "Senora, please tell me what will happen in thirteen years." Her poncho fell from her head and revealed a face of mystical Indian beauty framed by long black hair. Her deep, penetrating look sent shivers up my spine.

She spoke and the boy translated. "I do not understand everything the woman is telling me. She says that when you danced on the Pyramid of the Sun, the sun's glow entered your body and gave light to your blood. This will change your mind in thirteen years and you will enter into a new season."

"Now I am really confused," I said. "Listen young man. Please tell the woman that I thank her and ask if I can pay her for the flute."

"No," said the boy. "The woman will take no money."

"Thank you, thank you," I said. I began to walk away, then stopped to ask, "Why did the woman leave her home and come to Teotihuacan?"

The boy spoke to the woman, then said to me, "The woman says she has come to meet with the gods. They will come soon, and she will leave with them."

"What do you mean, leave with them? Do you mean that she is going to die?"

The boy looked at the woman, then said, "Yes." The rain stopped falling, and suddenly a bright sun broke over the boy's drenched head and his Mexican heritage shone on his wet face.

"Why does the woman think the gods will come to Teotihuacan and not to her home?"

"Because the woman believes that Teotihuacan is where the gods come when they come to earth."

My elbow slipped and jerked my hand from where it held my head. I started up, then looked out the office window at the hibiscus bush. What was happening to me? Why so many head trips and why such a clear review of a happening in Mexico nine years ago? It would be another four and a half years before something would happen, *if* it would happen.

I walked out of my office into the conference room. "Emily, I'm going home."

"You look beat, George, you should get some rest." Emily said.

"Nice to have you with us, Karen," I said.

From the far corner of the room Karen lifted her head from her work. "Thank you, Mr. Jonas." The sun sifted through the blinds and a few rays lit Karen's face, giving her a pure angelic beauty that made me pause and stare. Her long brown hair draped down across the right side of her shoulder and rested just above her bosom. Her brown eyes gleamed, and her innocent smile lent charm to a motherly figure. Were Karen not married, could I love her as I loved Despina? Would I be capable of love's expression, a tender touch? Would we have exciting conversation and companionship?

Questions filled my empty heart as I searched the unknown with the strong light of memory. My thoughts and behavior disturbed me. "Good-bye," I said, and rushed home. When I arrived, I wondered why I had rushed so. I really did not want to be at home, but I had nowhere else to go. Someone and something was missing, yet it also was not missing. I felt strange, but I didn't know why. The feeling was just there.

The wet bar was cluttered with empty wine bottles and dirty glassware. I looked at the liquor on the bar, debating which brand I would attack first. My eyes fell on the Cossart Rainwater Madeira. What a coincidence. Rainwater had fallen and been absorbed by my body, clear pearls of rainwater flowed into a flower and I had drunk it; and now before me was a Rainwater Madeira to soothe my feelings. As my palate identified the nectar of the gods, I remembered something that happened a few years ago. Glass in hand, I phoned a friend in Boston.

"Robert, this is George. I am sitting here with a glass of Rainwater Madeira thinking of the afternoon we both got smashed on Rainwater Madeira at the Bayou Room downstairs from the Two-Nineteen Restaurant in Alexandria. Tell me the truth Robert. Did you ever tell anyone about that afternoon?"

"Are you kidding, George? That experience will accompany me to my grave."

"We learned a few things from that experience, didn't we?"

"We sure did. I learned not to get zapped with a crazy philosopher."

"Hey! I wasn't that far gone, and I was correct in my analysis, wasn't I?"

"You sure were; you sure were. How did we ever stand outside the Two-Nineteen Restaurant on King Street, take off our shoes and ties and beg for money as if we were paupers? It had to be the Rainwater Madeira."

"I did not take off my tie. If you'll recall, you argued that one could beg more money by portraying a man poor in spirit than a man inspired by enthusiasm. You messed up your hair, took off your Italian-made shoes, removed the hideous tie you were wearing, opened your shirt three buttons down to expose a hairless chest, and transformed a dynamic, positive smile into a warped, dejected, depressing grimace to prove your stereotypical beggar could collect more money begging than the enthusiastic man I was going to portray. You should have been an actor."

"Why did we decide to beg in the street?" Robert asked. "Oh, I remember. We were about to lose all our money in the silver futures market, weren't we?"

"Yeah. We were both holding silver futures contracts, and the price had fallen two dollars per ounce. We stopped to have a drink and I said that it wouldn't bother me if I went broke and had to beg in the streets, because I wouldn't beg as a pauper, a man poor in spirit, but with enthusiasm, with a spirit proclaiming success, not failure. You said I wouldn't collect one penny that way and I said I would collect more than you. After half a dozen Rainwater Madeiras, we challenged one another. You took the role of a poor man, opened your shirt and acted tipsy. You begged for quarters, and I begged for dollars. I played the role of a rich man about to lose it all. I wore my tie and shoes and begged people for money. One couple gave me three dollars."

"I don't remember that," Robert said.

"Sure you do. We talked about the most anyone had given us."

"Three dollars, huh?"

"That's right. I asked people for money so I could buy the Wall Street Journal because I was about to lose all my money in the silver market. People laughed, then willingly gave me money.

"And what did we learn?"

"We learned not to be poor in spirit. We learned that people would rather help us achieve success than feed us or buy us a cup of coffee. People relate to success because they want it too. They resent the poor in spirit, the downtrodden, for it signifies failure, and they want no part of failure. That's why I collected more money than you did, Robert." We laughed together, remembering the moment. "Hey, Robert, I want to thank you and Arthur for coming down to Hilton Head to be with me when I needed your friendship."

"George, Despina was my surrogate mother. She was an important influence in my life. I love her and I miss her."

I fell silent. Tears flowed from my eyes and fell into my glass of Rainwater Madeira.

"George, are you all right?" Robert asked.

"Yes, I am all right. I am on the outside but poor in spirit within. I wonder if that's how a true beggar feels."

"No, that's different. A beggar tells himself he's poor in spirit for he has no money at that moment. Your spiritual poverty comes from losing a loved one. Knowing Despina, you may be disturbing her by thinking and feeling the way you do now. Pull yourself together, my friend."

"Robert, when you and Arthur were down here I had the opportunity to walk the fairway behind my house with him one late afternoon. We were walking and talking about business when I said, 'Arthur, do you see that tree to the left of the green about 100 yards from here?' He said he saw it. 'Well, in the early evenings, as the sun was setting, Despina and I would walk to that tree holding hands."

Arthur turned abruptly to me and said, "You held hands with Despina. You walked in the evening on this beautiful fairway to that tree. What beautiful moments you have had. So, what are you unhappy about? You've had it all. Most people never have anything like that. They're miserable, unhappy and out of love most of their married lives."

I looked at him and said, "I am sorry, Arthur."

His friendly, distinguished face smiled sadly. 'The relationship you had with Despina was special.' Robert, I felt badly. Robert, are you still there?"

"I am here."

"Are you listening?"

"Yes, go on, tell me."

"Robert, are you crying?"

"No, no, I've got a runny nose."

"Robert, you're fuckin' crying, aren't you?"

"Yeah, I am. I miss Despina. She was always there for me, like I was her son. I could talk for hours with her and she'd listen."

"You know, Robert, I see that now. I never realized that one of the reasons her girlfriends flocked to our house was because they liked talking with her. I always thought she was minding everybody's business."

"Hell no, Despina was a listener. There was something about Despina that made you tell her everything, like in a confession. She was a very trusting person. She'd make you laugh about how silly you were for taking your problem so seriously. Then, if you were really stupid about your problem, she'd call you a mishugana or a ganzmacher."

"Robert, that's funny; that's classic!"

"Well, it's true."

"Christ, I know she was a listener, but I never thought of Despina in that way."

"That's because it was always there with you. To an outsider, it made a striking first impression."

I gulped down the rest of the Rainwater Madeira, and as the sensation burned my larynx, guilt burned my mind. Had I lived with Despina for thirty years without knowing and appreciating her fine qualities? "Robert, if I ever had to write about Despina, I'd draw a blank. All I can think of and feel is her love. All I have ever known is her love. I don't know how not to be loved. I feel like a babe in the woods. Night after night I come home to nothing, to emptiness. I can't seem to handle it. My mind plays games with me. I make things up and pretend they have happened."

"What kind of things?"

"Well, I saw a nurse in the hospital when Despina was in coma. I only saw her for a few minutes, but she keeps coming into my mind. I imagine her feeling sorry for me and holding my head against her bosom."

"For Christ's sake, George, why don't you go back to the hospital and find that nurse?"

"I can't do that, Robert. I may be crazy, but I'm not totally insane. Besides, that was months ago."

"George, you need to get yourself together. In fact, you need to get laid."

"That's not what I need or want. I need to fill my heart with love's emotion. I need Agape."

"You had that with Despina. It's gone now; you may or may not have it again. What you are trying to do is to bring back or replace Despina. That's impossible. Just go out without expectations and meet someone. Can you do that? You can even place an ad in the singles column."

"Are you nuts? An ad in the singles column?"

"What's wrong with that? It could read 'Man with big puzo needs woman with Agape' "

"You're gonzo, Robert!"

"Better yet, put an ad in a woman's magazine: 'If you're a crazy woman, alone, and have money, you can have companionship and love and travel the world and have fun with a crazy philosopher.' Seriously, George, place an ad in the singles' column."

"I'll think about it," I said.

"Don't think about it — do it!"

"I have to run now, I'll talk with you tomorrow." And so we'd laughed, then cried, for the love that was Despina and the legacy of love she left behind. I poured myself another glass of Madeira, then walked out of the house to watch the beauty of the setting sun. The giant oak tree supported me, and I leaned against it. "Oh, giant oak," I whispered. "What is happening to me?"

My thoughts had traveled a hundred thousand miles that day from a definition of love to a disruption of my business to the pyramids in Mexico. Birds sang hymns in praise of divine love, and the giant oak told me to close my eyes, face the setting sun, and with the power of mind create a light. The light will show the way to transformation.

I gazed with awe at the giant oak. Had the tree transmitted thought to me? Had I heard it speak? I placed my hand on its thick bark and looked up into the limbs that seemed to reach to the heavens. Spanish moss gave character and individuality to the old oak, made it unique and set it apart from surrounding trees. A golden aura crowned it, as it absorbed energy from the sun's last rays. Soon the light of day faded.

A quick chill, then a hot flash ran up my spine. I felt the giant oak's energy before the darkness took hold. I went into the house, and with the bottle of Rainwater Madeira went to my bedroom and threw myself on my bed.

With my eyes closed, I called out to Despina. "Come to me, come talk to me." I lifted the bottle of Rainwater to my lips and attempted to swallow a mouthful while lying down. The Rainwater poured all over me. Laughing and crying at the same time, tired and crazy, I said, "Look, Despina, Rainwater has fallen all over me." The bottle soon fell from my grip and I was asleep.

My body felt heavy laying there. My mind was a crystal ball I could see into. A white light brightened and somehow I knew it to be a thought process, a dream of something real and yet unreal. An experience of the past or a happening in the present or something yet to arrive. The face of the Mayan woman appeared and I heard the boy say, "The sun's glow has entered your body and gives light to your blood and this will change your mind in thirteen years, and you will enter a new season."

As the woman's face faded, the oak tree called. "Your mind

will create a light and the light will help you understand your transformation."

Blood flowed swiftly through my veins, providing electrical energy to fuel the bright white light. I could not reason; all I could do was see the light and feel a deep, heavy feeling. And so the night went on until my heart began to beat so rapidly it awakened my sleeping body. Then the light in my mind faded, and as my mind fell into sleep I awakened.

I sat up on the edge of the bed. My feet touched the floor, my eyes focused on a night light at the far end of the bathroom. I felt numb, spaced out, unable to lift myself from where I sat. I kept staring at the night light as if it meant something more to me, as if I had known it before but could not determine where or when. The light began to flicker, images appeared and disappeared, and I thought I saw Despina lift her nightgown and sit on the toilet seat. "How do you feel?" I asked.

"Fine; I feel better," she said.

I then realized that this scene had taken place months ago, just before she fell into coma. I kept staring at the night light. I felt that I was moving, a different kind of movement, not physical but mental, a thought in motion somewhere out in space. "Oh, God," I cried out. "What are these strange thoughts and happenings that penetrate the levels of thought within my mind? They seem to surface from the deep well of love's emotion, brought on by the absence of love. These thoughts and feelings weigh heavy on my heart and mind.

"What is the source of the energy that lights my mind, that transmit my thoughts into the cosmos on a beam of light? What lights the depths of my psyche while my body sleeps? When my body awakens, what fuels its activity and thought process? Oh, God! Tell me, what is love? What is death?"

Three months passed. For me, it was a simple moment: a rising sun in the morning's glory, coming up from the ocean's horizon, to a setting sun in a golden aura of glory, fading beyond the island marsh.

Pat and I became friends. He worked with great effort to find a buyer for our company. He was concerned, however, for he was witnessing new disruptions to our distribution. Of the half dozen potential buyers for Masterbrand, three groups were ready to enter into a purchasing agreement, but Famous Ice Cream and its new-found management discovered ways to frighten them off.

"George, I am witness to the willful, deceptive, unfair acts of the Famous Ice Cream Company," Pat told me.

My work life became tense and stressful, full of fear and worry. What would happen to my son and daughter were I to be driven out of business? I knew I shouldn't worry. D'Ann was married to a responsible man. John was a very capable and knowledgeable young businessman. I could return to Boston. Bullshit! No one was going to destroy my business or my family. We'd have suffered and lost enough. I vowed to fight to the end for what was right and what was mine. Such were my daily thoughts. Putting the negatives aside, forging ahead with positive affirmations for success, John and I worked twice as hard and twice as long developing of our distribution, while Peterson kept reassuring me that I had nothing to worry about, and I continued to believe him.

At day's end, I would return home wanting and not wanting to spend the evening there. Nights without companionship, eating and drinking late into the night, falling into uneasy sleep, changed my body and metabolism. I began to gain weight; my heart beat rapidly and irregularly in the morning; I had no sleep until the following night. Then one morning I awakened with severe back pains. I went to a chiropractor. After receiving a minor back adjustment, I was sent to see a physical therapist for massage treatments.

How complex is the phenomena of thought. For months my thoughts rose from the hollow depths of loneliness. I would reflect on past experiences with Despina, mentally replaying our tragedy and my meaningless glance into an unknown nurse's green eyes. A woman in white on an elevator, a collision of thought, a simple moment enjoying a sensuous pleasure, the thought of a bosom to cry on. Suddenly, there stood before me that same nurse, my chiropractor's physical therapist. My face turned red. I wanted to run out of the building, but her pleasant smile and melodic "hello" held me.

"How have you been, Mr. Jonas?" she wanted to know.

"I've been all right. Do you know me?" I pretended that I had no memory of her.

"Everyone in Hilton Head Hospital knows of you and of your tragic loss. Please follow me."

"Pardon me, nurse, may I know your name?"

"Laurie."

We entered a small room set up for masotherapy. "Miss Laurie —"

"Not Miss Laurie, just Laurie."

"Laurie, I have never had a woman massage me before, I feel uneasy."

"Take off your clothes, everything except your shorts, then lie on this table," she instructed, paying no mind to what I had said. She threw a sheet over my mid-section and I lay there with my eyes closed in total embarrassment. Warm oil in her soft hand moved up and down my left arm. It felt good.

I kept my eyes closed, thinking about how wonderful a woman's hand felt. There was strength in the fingers pushing blood into my muscles and a warm tenderness in the palm of her hand. A woman was touching me for the first time in over a year, and it had been a long time since I'd touched a woman. I felt myself rise and harden. Concerned and abashed I lifted my head, opened my eyes, and saw her acknowledge the rise beneath the sheet.

"I think we need a little music. I love Bach's violin concertos as played by Isaac Stern. Keep your eyes closed; this should relax you." Laurie pushed my head back onto the pillow, then leaned over me pushing the flesh of my chest upward. The warmth of her breath on my face was like a passionate kiss. Occasionally, her breast touched me, but only slightly. However slight it might have been, to me it became a series of explosively sensuous thoughts. I opened my eyes again in an attempt to change my thoughts, only to find myself staring into the green eyes I had clashed with on the elevator so many months ago.

"Relax. Close your eyes, George," Laurie said. She called me George; her breast touched me; I wonder if she likes me? My mind continued to run with each movement of her hands on my body. The tender touch, the sensation, the new found reality, the emotional fulfillment arising from sorrow all sought expression in a realization of love.

The hour-long massage from Laurie, a nurse, a masseuse, a physical therapist, made me feel thin and tall. Blood moved within my body; my yin and yang were in synchronicity. My aura was re-energized by the circular motions of Laurie's hands eight inches above my body.

"When this timer goes off in five minutes," Laurie said, "you can get dressed."

"Laurie, we've met before today."

"I know. It was at the hospital. Now close your eyes and relax." She left the room.

I lay there feeling different. Moments later, I got up from the massage table, dressed and walked to the front office. Laurie was speaking to a woman in Spanish who had been in to see the chiropractor. When the woman left I approached Laurie.

Her golden brown hair was pulled back in a ponytail, revealing a long lean neck supporting a beautiful head. Her face was scarred by hardships which toughened her, but her green eyes contrasted with her white, soft cheeks and lent her an angelic beauty. My eyes fell on her breasts, and I experienced once again the wanting. The man and the child within me hungered for her.

"How do you feel, George?" Laurie asked.

"I feel great," I said. I gazed at her face, studied its profile. Her lips were wide and heart-shaped, her lower lip full and sensuous, her upper lip thin and intellectual.

I paid and scheduled another visit in two days. Feeling great, I drove straight home. I thought about having a drink but decided not to, especially since Laurie had told me that the soreness of my back muscles was from excessive drinking, not from physical strain. Savannah Lady was with John, and I found myself alone once again. This time, however, there was a difference. I had something else I could think about. I could think of Laurie instead of tragedy. I could think of the potential of love and an affair with Laurie. I sat sipping a glass of water and listening to swingtime on the radio. It made me blue. What right did I have to assume that a one-hour massage from a nurse fifteen years my junior meant anything? Why would a beautiful and thin woman want to have anything to do with an overweight, tired, troubled older man? Hey, why not, I demanded. I was a man's man. I got up from my chair and began trying on my suits and jackets. None fit. I fell back onto my bed, kicked off my pants and just lay there, depressed.

I hugged my pillow, closed my eyes, and thought of Laurie. Vividly I felt her leaning over me, her breast touching me. I felt her rubbing my fingers and the palm of my hand. I had an enormous erection. Taking hold, I began to massage myself, transferring the sensation of the massage, the thought of Laurie rubbing my hand now unreal, into a present sensation, which was real. I never thought I was performing; it was Laurie rubbing and stroking. Then, with a clear and vivid picture of Laurie in my mind, I had an explosive orgasm. Intellectual realism and the intense sexual pleasure came together and I cried out, "Oh, God! Thank you for this moment."

The experience found the lost man in me, and I came alive. I felt the need to know Laurie, to have her as a friend, if not a lover. Robert might be right. He had advised me to pursue a friendship with someone. With great courage, I phoned her office. Unfortunately, she had left for the day. Disappointed, I started talking aloud to myself.

"George, do you know what you are doing? What's happening to you? You go for a simple massage, meet this lady, Laurie, whom you met briefly once before on an elevator, come home, hack off and behold, you now believe it a psychic phenomena."

"Yeah, George, I think you're going fuckin' bananas," I told myself as I looked into the mirror.

I was beginning to doubt myself again, be negative, find reasons not to rather than find reasons to do what I so badly wanted to do.

"To hell with it! I need someone to talk to. I'll pursue a friendship with the woman. I'll write to her and tell her my innermost thoughts, let her come to know me. I'll hand deliver the letter when I go for therapy.

Pen in hand, I set out to consign to paper the thoughts overflowing my mind.

Dear Laurie:

If these words are heavy with love, forgive me! I have a problem. I don't know what it is not to be loved. All I have ever known is love and companionship. Despina filled my heart and home with love. How fortunate a man I have been, but the gods punished me and took beautiful Despina away from me. I have come to know only loneliness and the hardship it has created for me. For months I screamed, cried and kicked like a spoiled brat. I locked myself in the house, drank bottle after bottle of wine, argued with the gods about their judgment. Why, I asked, did you strip me naked of this emotion called love and replace it with the emotions of death, grief and torment? Did I not love her as she loved me? Did I not keep her warm in my embrace? Did I not with gentleness thrust myself deep within her womb and bring her to heights that glorified love? Did I not look into her eyes in those precious moments and identify with her psyche?

A nice, quiet feeling came over me as I wrote. It felt good. I paused to read what I had written. My God, what kind of crazy letter was I attempting to write and deliver to a woman I didn't know? I was going out of my mind. It would be better, when I go for my next appointment, to ask her to dinner like a normal man would.

Again, I reread my letter. Why did I refer to gods rather than to God? Why did I repeat that I didn't know what it was not to be loved? How could I explain to anyone my state of mind? And if I could, would anyone understand it? Although I realized the letter was out of order, it felt good to have written it. My thoughts continued to flow, and I continued to write as love's emotion grew within me.

And a voice responded, "Too long in your life you have taken love for granted. Love was given to you, for Despina possessed it and therefore you shared it. Now that it is no longer, you weep like a child for it. Think of her loneliness when she waited for you to return. Cry not for what has happened to you; cry for what has happened to Despina."

"Oh, infinite intelligence, bring her to me that I may fall to my knees and kiss her feet in adoration. Bring her to me that I may touch her cheek and gaze on her face with love and adoration."

The voice responded. "Your adoration for Despina will be expressed in your love for another, for one who has need of your love."

And I asked, "But how will I find and know such a woman?"

And the voice said, "She will come to you as fallen rain. It shall be written on her brow. You will fall to her, knowing by her warm and friendly manner as she eases the pain of your wounds that her heart and mind will open to you in your need.

"She will be a woman who has been made love to but who was never loved by those she has tried to embrace. Like Despina, she will be earthly, spirited, and humorous. She will want to know you, yet she will reject you in the same moment. Your need to know her love for you must not be desperate.

"Cultivate her as you would a rosebud and, just before the bloom of her flower, pluck her from her stem and breathe deeply of her fragrance. Bring her your lips and kiss the softness of her petals. Though she may struggle to deny you, you will notice her comfort in your embrace. Hold her tightly, do not let her go, for your embrace is truly what she needs.

"Your journey will be difficult and not one for half a man. Acknowledge her and she will help you become the whole man you can be. She will unfold and yield to you. Tears will flow from her eyes and her longing for true love will be no more. Thus, your adoration for Despina will be expressed in your love and caring for another, for one who has need of your love."

I walked to the stereo, inserted a Sinatra tape and felt the mood. Although my words were genuine and from deep within, I felt somewhat embarrassed for having written them. I was about to discard the pages when a new feeling came over me, and I believed that my words were an expression of love for Despina and that I should save them. I was beginning to believe that what I had written would become a reality.

During the next two days, I read my notes over and over, embedding in my mind that what I had written was truth. It was going to happen with Laurie. This woman I hardly knew would ease my pain with her hands. I would surrender to her warm and friendly manner. She was the rainwater that would fall on my naked body. She was the rainwater that would enter my blood stream and carry love into my empty heart. She was the unknown face in the flower's heart. Knowing and believing Marcus Aurelius' dictum that "whatever the mind of man can conceive and believe, man will achieve," I kept my therapy appointment with Laurie. And with each press of her hands on my body, the movement of blood relaxed my muscles. A light lit in my mind. The written thoughts of the unreal became the real, and the fiction became the fact.

My hand trembled as I wrote the check for my therapy session. "Laurie, please have dinner with me this Saturday," I said.

Her eyes lightened to a bright translucent jade, opening the corridors of her mind. I was thrown back by a glance that hit me like a bolt of lightning. In soft voice, Laurie said, "I would love to have dinner with you, George." she said.

My knees buckled. I attempted to stand straight, as I gazed in astonishment at a woman with an angelic smile who had humbly accepted my dinner invitation. "Where do you live? I'll pick you up," I offered.

"No, that's fine. Let's meet in the lounge at the Hyatt in Palmetto Dunes."

We arranged to meet at six in the evening, and I left quickly. The bright glare of the sun blinded me as I walked toward my car. I was excited. My heart beat rapidly. Blood flooded my head; my thoughts jostled with one another as I drove home. "Oh, Despina, I long to hold you in my arms," I whispered, but then I thought, if I could hold Laurie close to me, feel her warmth, close my eyes, might I transmit my thoughts to Despina? Would she receive them? Could I pretend Laurie was Despina for a simple moment in love's embrace? Would that be fair to Laurie? Wouldn't that be using her? Should I ask Laurie if I could use her that way? Would she be insulted if I held her and asked her to allow me to pretend I was holding someone else? It would satisfy my desperate need to embrace Despina a final time, to kiss her farewell and good-by.

Could I be capable of love with Laurie? Could I love her with my heart and mind? Wasn't I experiencing love now? What were these feelings? Were they emotions of love or feelings of insecurity from being alone? I thought I could make love to Laurie, but then again, maybe not. She was the first woman to come into my life since Despina's passing. Christ, I've had only a slight acquaintance with Laurie, a mere meeting. Why was I putting myself through this mental hell? No, wait, there was something different about Laurie. I'd thought about her for a year after only a brief encounter on an elevator. Could one, should one, fall in love with the first person one meets after the loss of a loved one? Would that "love" come from a broken heart or unsound mind?

I wondered how Laurie saw me? She had accepted my dinner invitation; maybe she needed me. I wondered if she'd ever been married. That didn't matter. I had to make her understand me. Perhaps I should read my notes to her so she would know me. Then again, maybe I shouldn't. She might think I was out of my mind, fuckin' nuts.

How could I rid myself of this confusion, this trail of thought in quest of knowledge of the emotion called love. Could I, with calm reasoning, ease the discomfort caused by my emotions?

"That's it!" I thought. "I'll create a thought process, an analytical formula, so the rational and dialectical, will remove the pain and torment from my mind and relieve me from the pain of having lost my psyche's companion."

Never ending thoughts, conversations with myself, my internal monologue went on and on. I experienced the dinner date a hundred times before it actually took place. The actual experience of the dinner date joined the speculative thoughts about the experience and when the time came I was late. I looked for Laurie in the lounge. Had she left in a huff? Then I saw her. Her golden brown hair was full, brushed out and gracefully appealing. Her light blue dress softened her green eyes, which sparkled like jewels in a blue sky. With a warm smile, she greeted me and kissed me on the cheek. I kissed her cheek. She took my arm and led me to her table. I was comforted by her taking hold of my arm. She was friendly and sincere, and I felt something special when she wrapped her arm around mine. After a brief but warm conversation and a drink, we decided to have dinner at Alexander's Restaurant in Palmetto Dunes.

184

"Laurie, thank you for coming to dinner with me. What will you have to drink?"

"Oh, a glass of red wine."

"Bring us the Mondavi Cabernet Special Reserve," I instructed the waiter. "I think you'll like this wine, Laurie."

"It's a fine wine," agreed the waiter before leaving.

"Tell me about yourself, Laurie."

"No, you tell me about you first." We both laughed childishly.

"I'll tell you, then you tell me; I'll tell you something, then you tell me something," I sang. Laurie laughed and we both became silly. "Christ, we haven't had any wine yet, and already we're acting funny."

"It's the gin martinis we had at the hotel before coming here. 'Shake instead of stir, with three big Spanish olives.' That was cute, George."

I took hold of her hand, pressed gently and she responded by pressing back. "Laurie, the warmth from your hand was felt by my heart,"

"That was just the martini arriving home," she laughed.

"I don't care what it is. I am enjoying your companionship. I am proud to be with you, and I'm happy in a way that I haven't been in a very long time."

Laurie sat up straight, held the stem of her wine glass as the waiter poured the wine. Her eyes moved to my glass, and she watched the wine pour into it before raising her eyes to meet with mine, and then I saw into her mind. She too was lonely. She had been betrayed by a lover.

"To you, lovely lady, and I thank you for this gracious moment," I toasted. Our glasses rang and we sipped our wine.

"Ah," she sighed, "there is nothing like a good wine."

"Laurie, I've known loneliness and I see a loneliness in you that's shadowed by a sadness caused by one you have loved."

"Good Lord, what have I here? A psychic?"

"No, I am not a psychic. I just had a feeling; I just sensed it."

"Yeah, but that was too close to home. It was right on. I am here to enjoy the evening with you, to forget my loneliness, my sadness."

"And I am here for the same reason, and I want to treasure each moment, be happy, say the right things, but please bear with me just a little. Being out on a dinner date is new to me. You are young, intelligent, and beautiful; me, I am older and somewhat philosophical. Needless to say, your time is of another dimension. I live in one world, you another, yet the weather is the same and so are our feelings of loneliness and the discomfort from the emotions of love."

"Boy, this is going to be some evening."

I lifted my glass of wine and toasted her. "To you, Laurie, my new friend."

"And to you," she replied, "my new friend for a long, long time."

Within that short a period of time, a special feeling and the warmth of friendship had surfaced, comforting if only for the moment, two lonely people.

How could I ever have thought that I might remove the pain and torment from my mind, the absent feeling, through reason and deduction? It wasn't that I had forgotten my plight but that a new emotion had cloaked the old one. Warm friendship comforted me and filled the void, overcoming the feelings of absence.

"Well, are you going to tell me about you?"

"I don't know what to say."

"Oh, come on now, say anything."

186

"Well, I'll tell you about who I am today, O.K?"

"All right, Mr. Mysterious."

"It's just that for the past year, I have been kind of crazy. I see lights in my mind. I'm spaced out, somewhere on the fifth floor."

"After what you've been through, that seems normal. How is your business doing?"

"Business is great. I was having a problem with Famous Ice Cream, but they've reassured me that I have nothing to worry about. Now, tell me about you."

"Let's see. I got divorced eight years ago; I have two children: a nine-year-old boy and a twelve-year-old girl. Then I met a man from Ireland. We fell in love, and I married him. Six months later, he split — ran off with another woman. My second divorce will soon be finalized. I hold two jobs to make ends meet, one as a nurse, the other as a physical therapist and masseuse. Enough of what we're about. You promised to tell me a Greek myth."

"A Greek myth, *hmm*. Do you know why we have an echo?"

"No. Why?"

"Well, there was once a woman who would not stop talking. She would talk, and talk and never listen to anyone else. Her name was Echo. The gods became angry with her so they decided to silence her, except for the last two words in each sentence. She continued to talk, and talk, but all anyone could hear were her last two words. That is why we have an echo. Silly, isn't it?"

"No, I love it. Tell me another."

"O.K. Do you know how the flower narcissus got its name?"

"No."

"Well, once there was a handsome young man named Narcissus. At the very break of dawn each day, he would run to a pool of water and look into it for hours to admire his reflection. He fell in love with his own reflection, and the gods punished him by transforming him into a flower. They named the flower Narcissus. Today narcissism means self-love; admiration of one's self."

"That's cute. How about a myth with more drama?"

"O.K., one more, but that's it. Promise?"

"I promise."

"In a small village, living in adjoining parts of a single dwelling, were two families. One family had a son, the other a daughter. The children were forbidden to see or speak to one another because their families hated one another. The duplex was separated by a center wall and the beds of the young man and woman were on opposite sides of this wall.

"These young people loved one another, but their families kept them apart, so they dug a small hole in the wall through which they exchanged notes. At night, they pressed their lips against the hole in the wall so the passion of their love could be felt. One night, unable to bear being apart any longer, they decided to run away together. They arranged to meet under the white mulberry tree near the edge of the forest. The girl left her home first. The boy was supposed to follow soon after, but something delayed him. Darkness overtook the light of day, and frightened by the sound of a lion's roar, the girl ran away from the mulberry tree. Her white shawl fell from her shoulders and was torn to shreds by a wounded lion. When the boy arrived at the mulberry tree, he found a torn, blood stained silk shawl. He called for his love, and ran around the white mulberry tree where he found other torn garments with blood stains. He fell to his knees, crying out to the gods that he could not live without the girl he loved. Then he drew his sword and thrust it into the pit of his stomach. He fell dead on the ground.

"Moments later, the terrified young woman found her way back to the mulberry tree where she found her loved one dead, the torn shawl in his hand. 'I cannot live without you!' She screamed and pulled the sword from his stomach and threw herself on it. She fell dead on top of her lover, and the blood from both lovers was absorbed into the earth. The roots of the mulberry tree drank the blood and the white mulberry turned red, which is what gives the mulberry its distinctive color."

"Oh, George, that was beautiful."

"Women in my heyday never thought so. In fact, that story usually scared them away."

"Well, I loved it. Love isn't understood today the way it was in times past. You also might have scared them away for other reasons."

"I believe I know what love is, Laurie, for I have always had love in my life. My concern now is to bring it back into my life, back into my heart and my soul. The question is, will it be true love or a disguised need that I will accept out of desperation to fill my empty heart?"

I reached over and took her hand. She had a serious look on her face that I could not interpret. Her green eyes stared directly into mine. Had I upset her? Was I coming on too strong? The moment of silence, was broken by a bolt of lightning that snapped at the earth. A shocking, thunderous sound followed. Outside, the lagoon reflected the sudden white light and blessed our friendship. Then the rain fell hard.

"The gods approve of our friendship," I said. We laughed and clicked our wine glasses. We stared into one another's eyes and drank to the god of wine.

"You speak Spanish, don't you?"

"How did you know?"

"I heard you talking to a patient. But you're not Spanish, are you?"

"No, I am French, Polish and a little bit of everything else."

"Ever been to Mexico?"

"Many times, but I prefer Belize and the Yucatan. Have you been to Belize or the Yucatan?"

"No I haven't. Just Mexico."

"You should go."

"Laurie, what does 'maia' mean?"

"It means the month of May. It's also the name of a Greek or Roman goddess. I don't remember which."

"How did you come to learn Spanish?"

"Spanish is necessary if one is to be an effective nurse."

"You're quite knowledgeable."

"Not really. I will admit to having studied pre-Columbian art and Central American Civilization."

"Where?"

"University of Mexico. Two semesters."

"Really? That must have been exciting."

"It was."

"What is Central American Civilization?"

"It's a study of the cultures of the Aztec, Toltec, and Mayan civilizations."

"Did you say Mayan?" When she nodded, I said, "That's it, Laurie. You were meant to be for me."

"What?! Cool it, George."

Feeling rejected, I sat quietly, and stared into my glass of red wine. I wanted something to happen to me. When I looked up, I saw kindness on Laurie's face.

"Why did you want to know about the word 'maia'?"

"It's a long story, Laurie."

"Oh, come on now, tell me. I am having so much fun, just talking, just being here with you."

"It's a nightmare, Laurie."

"That's all right. You can tell me."

She pulled my hand into both of hers and pressed firmly. She rubbed her strong fingers into my palm; her thumbs pressed against the base of my thumb.

"Laurie, when you massage my hand like that, you awaken the man in me."

"Are you talking about the little guy that pushed up the sheet the other day?" She fell back into her seat roaring with laughter.

My face turned beet red. "It's not supposed to wake the man in you, George; it's to relax you, calm you down."

I smiled shyly. Christ, she saw the lump beneath the sheet when she first gave me a massage. And what was this about 'the little guy?' What did she mean by that? I'd have to watch what I said to women these days.

"All right now, you tell me why you wanted to know about 'maia' and why you were troubled by it."

She sat up and looked attentively at me. Instead of a skeptical scholar, I saw a figure of delicate femininity and my mind and heart opened. I wanted desperately to know her. "O.K., I'll tell you. It all started when I danced on a pyramid."

"You danced on a Pyramid?" Laurie laughed, choked on the wine she was drinking, coughed and laughed some more. "Excuse me, George. I have to go to the little girls' room."

"Are you all right?"

"You made me laugh so hard I have to pee."

"Oh." I watched her stagger off and wondered why she thought I was so funny. I'm not funny. In fact, I'm a very serious person. Christ, was I out of it? Laurie was different from other women I'd known. I wondered what it would be like to make love to her. While I was pondering this, she returned.

"I promise to take you very seriously this time. Now about maia…"

"Laurie, are you sure you want to hear this?"

"More than ever."

"About three months ago I was in my office, feeling depressed, and I thought of the time I went to Mexico with my family."

"When was that?"

"Nine years ago. We went to see the pyramids."

"Which pyramids?"

"Teotihuacan."

"I know them well."

"Anyway, a few weeks ago I had a dream, a flashback, really, in which I was dancing on a pyramid."

"Did you actually dance on a pyramid?"

"Yes, I did. In the rain. I danced and I danced, and I called out to God."

"What kind of dance?"

"Like Zorba or Tevye in "Fiddler on the Roof." It stopped raining on top of the pyramid, but continued to rain all around the pyramid. Then nine Indian men appeared." I hesitated. "Laurie, I never told this to anyone. Why are you laughing?" My companion was red in the face from laughing so hard that I thought she was going to fall off her chair.

"What the hell, Laurie," I said, disappointed.

"Please, George, don't stop. This is better than Greek mythology."

Reluctantly I continued. "Frightened, I ran down the pyramid. I was running down this long path — "

"The Street of the Dead?"

"What do you mean?"

"Was the pyramid one of the smaller ones?"

"No, it was the biggest and the tallest one."

"That was the Pyramid of the Sun. It leads into the Street of the Dead."

"Christ, Laurie, I think you're right. How did you know?"

"I've been there. I told you I'd studied Central American Civilization. What happened next?"

"Well, an Indian woman with a poncho over her head accompanied by a young Mexican boy stopped me while it was pouring rain. She called 'Maia, maia' to me. Then she gave me a flute."

"A what?"

"A flute. You know, the instrument you blow on. I offered her some money, but she wouldn't take it." I paused, unwilling to go on with my story. Laurie was laughing again and covering her face with her napkin to mask it. I was happy that she was laughing and having a good time, but I couldn't understand what was so funny. Then she stopped and a serious looking Laurie sat quietly, her hands clasped.

I had been about to tell her that our meeting was meant to be, but I thought that might be pushing it. "Laurie, after dinner let's go somewhere where we can hear music or even dance."

"I love to dance," Laurie said. A quick thought came to me: I would hold her in my arms, feel her warmth, realize the contour of her body, and transmit a thought to Despina. "You're thinking about Despina, aren't you, George?"

I was shocked. I did not realize that I had drifted away.

"I won't lie to you; there was a moment's thought of Despina. Have I offended you, Laurie?"

"Of course not," she said. She took hold of my hand and gave it a squeeze.

"Laurie, do you know anything about bananas?"

"Bananas! Now that is a classic case of changing the subject, but what do you want to know about bananas?"

"We'll talk about bananas another time. Are you enjoying the evening?"

"Very much. It is really different."

"In what way?"

"Well, I can't say I've ever been taken out to a fine, expensive restaurant by a gentleman who tells myths, and dances on pyramids."

"No, I guess not. Tell me, how do men treat women these days, and what do you do?"

"George, come closer," Laurie said. I leaned forward. "George, we fuck," she whispered.

I sat back in my chair, smiled and tried to sound nonchalant. "That's interesting." I didn't want her to know that she'd blasted me out of my chair.

"Things have changed, George. There are no feelings of love. People just have relationships and most of the time they are sexual relationships. 'I love you' doesn't mean what it did when you spoke those words to Despina. These days, when someone says, 'I love you,' I back off. I question his sincerity. I know he just wants to fuck me. So, I tell him, 'don't tell me you love me, just do me.' Do you want to fuck me, George?"

"No, Laurie; I want to love you."

"See, George, you can't accept a relationship with the word 'fuck' in it. That's all right. I can accept the sincerity of your word, 'love.' You are from a different era."

"Era! Christ, I'm not *that* much older than you."

"Well, maybe I should have said 'A different-thinking generation.' Today it's bullshit talk, loud hard rock, sensuous dance movement and a big hard cock. Am I being unladylike?"

"No, you are being honest. You're a very beautiful person, and I love you just the way you are. Don't change. I have my own madness to deal with. I have known loneliness, been desperate for love, and suffered an empty heart. I want to feel the tenderness of touch, to transmit the emotion physically. When I make love, I want to include the thought of a simple press of hands and the warmth of companionship to comfort my soul. I want it all, at the same time, working in harmony expressing love."

"George, I've only known you for a few hours, and I am troubled."

"Troubled? Aren't you having a pleasant evening?"

"Yes, I am, but that's not what I mean. I mean your words and the way you express love, and the emotion that you give off is very powerful, and that troubles me."

"I mean no harm. You're the first woman I have talked to in almost a year. I have a lot to express, emotionally."

"That's what I'm afraid of. I'm afraid of the emotion. I know I need it; it's natural. I'd probably be pouring out my own feelings if I could let go, but something in me won't allow it."

"Well, when you met the guy from Ireland and decided to marry him, didn't you feel love first?"

"This conversation is getting into an area I didn't want to get into, but I think I understand and can trust you, so I'll tell you. I was attracted to him physically. He was six years younger than me. He played the piano. He was good looking and impressive. As a lover, he was a stiff, but I thought I could develop him. He was good to my children and they liked him. I was lonely, so I married him. Then, he ran off with some bimbo. I now believe he married me so he could stay in this country."

"Laurie, a couple of days ago I had such deep feelings of withdrawal and the lack of love that I needed someone to come into my life, someone to love. It got so that I— I—"

"Did you say that you like to dance?" Laurie asked sprightly, knowing that I was about to confess something very personal. I was going to tell her how I had willed her into my life. She rescued me from making a fool of myself by her interruption.

"I love to dance, but I haven't in a very long time." We left the restaurant and drove to the Intercontinental Hotel in silence. As we entered, the music excited us, and we danced, talked, and danced some more. I held her gently and tightly.

"Laurie, my friend Robert said that I should put an ad in the singles column."

"That's not a bad idea, George."

"But now that I have you, I won't. Besides, that's not me."

"Slow down, George. You don't have me. This is our first date and I don't want to be owned as if I were a piece of property."

"I've known you for over a year, ever since I first saw you on the elevator in the hospital."

"Let's talk about that," she said as we danced romantically to easy music. "I'm a registered nurse and I have a pretty good idea of how the mind works. You were losing Despina then. Your infatuation was not real. It was a way of holding on to Despina. You couldn't accept the fact that she was in coma and about to die. When you saw me, you saw Despina. When she died, you couldn't let her go so you fixed me in your mind. You held onto a one-minute elevator ride for a whole year. Tell me the truth now: how long have you thought of me?"

"Honest, Laurie, I thought of you every other day for a whole year, but I saw and thought of Despina, too."

"You poured her into me in your mind, didn't you? You made me her shadow, didn't you?"

Instead of responding, I pulled Laurie into my embrace. We remained quiet, dancing beautifully to the smooth music. My face felt the warmth of her cheek, and my lips slid up and down her neck. I felt her breasts press into my chest. My right leg felt the heat of her inner thigh. Our movement was free; our rhythm, graceful; our embrace, romantic.

"George?"

"Yes, Laurie."

"I am sorry about what I said."

"There was some truth to it, Laurie."

"George, I think — "

"Yes, Laurie, tell me."

"I think, I could love you."

"Do you mean love like in the word 'love': emotionally, from within."

"Yes, George, I really mean from within."

I went berserk! My dream, the concept, the visualization had become reality. I remained outwardly quiet, but inwardly I felt crazy.

"Do you know what?" I whispered.

"What, George."

"You know, I believe we could make mad passionate love."

"That would be a big plus, George."

"That would be the best of both worlds, wouldn't it?"

Not once did I think of Despina, as I hoped and thought I would. Not once did I think of transmitting a thought in an effort to communicate with her. I just danced in passionate madness, sweating erotica, thinking of Laurie lying nude on my naked body, her nipples touching my nipples, our lips welded together, our tongues in rapid interpretation of sexual play. I saw her lying still on top of me, motionless except for our tongues, silent and still. I, deep within her womb, hard, fully erect could feel her pulse beat, could feel it pounding against me, while the intense heat from the walls of her womb incited me to even greater depth. Then the music stopped, the lights came on and my fantasy ended.

"George, I haven't had so much fun in a long time. Thank you, thank you so much."

The moon was full and a salty ocean breeze caressed us as we slowly walked to my car. We paused, leaned against the car, talked briefly about how well we had danced together. She kissed me on the cheek. I returned the kiss respectfully, then, without thinking, swiftly moved to her lips and pressed them gently, then pressed firmly, then passionately, I took hold of her lower lip with mine and with a swift thrust of my tongue entered her mouth. My lips moved to her ears, then down her neck. I opened her blouse, and my thoughts of a year ago came true. She wore no bra, and I gazed with adoration on her breasts. My lips embraced her nipples; I buried my face in her tender, soft magnificence. The man became the child.

"George, stop!" She pushed me away and tucked her breasts back into her blouse. I took a step back, astonished at my courage, my gall, to have been so bold. I wondered what to say or do next, although I felt good about what I'd done. I also felt bad about it, as if I had done Laurie a wrong. Had I gone too far? Was I desperate and unromantic? Had I embarrassed her? I know I felt embarrassed; in fact, I felt guilty about my ill- mannered attempt at seduction.

I said nothing, remained quiet, I comforted her with my embrace. She too was quiet, feeling secure within my arms. I realized she needed to be loved. She too was lonely and in need. The moon was high and bright, casting shadows that danced on the ocean breeze. The waves rolled in, snapping and breaking on the white sands.

We walked away from the car and down a path that led to the beach. We kicked off our shoes and with stocking feet ran foolishly on the tiny waves. She felt chilled, so I put my arm around her, rubbed her, sat her down and dried her feet with my jacket. I put my arms around her and leaned her back until she was lying down.

Abruptly she sat back up and said, "George, please stop. It's not the right time."

"I understand. Please just lie down and rest your head on my shoulder. Be in the warmth of my embrace. We'll look at the moon together. Let me hold you, simply hold you in my arms, in my embrace." Her green eyes looked at me sharply as she questioned my trustworthiness.

"It's all right, it's all right," I whispered.

We leaned back. She nested snugly in my arms, and her head rested comfortably on my shoulder. I pulled her closer to me, positioned my left leg between hers. She pressed her pelvis against me, wanting me. The white sand felt damp from the earlier rain, but the heat from our bodies obliterated any discomfort.

The moon hovering in the black sky glowed on the ocean. The glow rose to light the sky.

The heat from our bodies created an aura, influenced by the energy from the moon. The aura around our bodies generated a white light which lit our minds. The ocean sang subliminal messages, lifting us to higher realms in the universe. We held one another and remained quiet for the longest time.

"What are you thinking about, George?"

"Oh, crazy things."

"Tell me."

"No, they're way out."

"Oh, come on, talk to me."

"Well, when I look up at the big beautiful moon I see myself dancing on top of the Pyramid of the Sun in Mexico. I feel alone and wet from the rain. I see myself eating a dead pigeon my grandmother found in a cemetery. I see Uncle Nico feeding goats and Mr. Mike looking up at the sky and talking to his mother. Laurie, my mind is spinning with pictures and thoughts."

She placed her hand on my forehead. "You're warm, George, but you're all right. Just keep talking. Let it all come out. Talk to me. Tell me more."

"I hear a woman calling out, 'Maia, maia.' And a young boy telling me that the woman is saying that the sun's glow has entered my body and given light to my blood. And this will change my mind in thirteen years. Then I will enter a new season."

"The boy told you that?"

"Yes, nine years ago. It has come back to haunt me this year."

"It sounds like a riddle. It's mystical. George, are you familiar with the term, 'harmonic convergence'?"

"No, Laurie; what is it?"

"It may be a way of understanding the riddle."

"Tell me; I'm interested."

"From what you said about the sun rays entering your body and energizing your blood carrying new energy to your mind, I understand that in thirteen years you will complete your transformation. Have you felt any burning or sensations of heat?"

200

"I've had a burning feeling for you."

"I don't mean that kind of feeling, George."

"Then I guess I haven't. The only spaced-out experience I've had occurred with Despina's passing."

"What about your business difficulties?"

"Famous Ice Cream? They infuriate me. My spirits plunge and I'd feel airy-headed. I'd hear strange soft tones and sense things, just before they were about to happen. Add that to my depression, and it's a wonder I'm not out of my mind."

"George, these happenings, the feelings and the depression, have stimulated your brain. The sun's rays have entered your body, energized your blood, and it *will* change you. You're having a galactic experience. You're riding a galactic beam into the earth's core and interacting with the cosmic mind."

"You mean, I'm going bananas!"

"Oh, no, not at all. But my friend, Elizabeth, with whom I channel, is well versed in Mayan, mystical and paranormal thought. She'll be able to help you."

"What do you do with Elizabeth?"

"We belong to a channeling group."

"What's that?"

"We practice meditative thought and try to reach our spiritual guides."

"Oh, Laurie, you're so beautiful." I placed my hand on one side of her face. She pressed her cheek against it. "You have such wisdom. Will you love me with your heart and mind and let your psyche be my companion in love?" The clouds scudded across the moon and all was dark. Laurie's warm lips sought mine. I remained still and closed my eyes.

"Keep your eyes closed and relax. Think about anything and anyone you wish. Tell me about Despina."

"I can't; I don't know how."

"You must try. Talk to me."

"She was a rose among roses, beautifully formed and deeply red. Her fragrance, her caring, drifted with the wind."

Her fingers touched my lips and massaged my forehead. She pressed her fingers into my eye sockets and gently rubbed them. Her warm lips kissed my lips again and remained there. All was still and very quiet. Then I saw Despina in my mind. She came closer and closer, then kissed my lips, a gentle kiss. Laurie's lips were still on my lips, and Despina's lips were on my lips.

The earth beneath us shook. I trembled. Laurie lay still, locked within a moment in time. The past met the present. The real united with the unreal. Within love's embrace, the adoration in all its glory was sealed with a kiss. The clouds that masked the moonlight passed on. The sky glowed.

"Laurie, thank you, for this moment. I want to be honest with you; your kiss was Despina's kiss. When your lips were on mine, Despina came to me. She kissed me and I kissed her."

"I know. I felt her presence. She came through me to kiss you. I wanted to be there for both of you for what could be the final time."

"Since Despina's passing, I've longed for a final embrace." A tear fell on me and made its way to the corner of my mouth. "You're crying. Oh, my dear Laurie, what have I put you through this evening? I am so sorry."

"Don't be. I'm fine. It was just so beautiful. I feel so different. I think Despina left something in me, something good. I feel it."

"Come back into my arms as a friend. Let me hold you for another moment in love's embrace."

And I held her in my arms, and we fell on the white sands holding one another tightly as friends in love's embrace, fulfilling one another's desperate emotional needs. Then the moonlight faded once again. Thunder rumbled across the sky and rain fell. The ocean roared and darkness closed over us. I helped a frightened, lovely woman to her feet and we ran to the car.

THE END (BOOK ONE)

I personally thank you for reading this book.

George D. Manjounes

Also in memory of John David Granger, Sr. of Americus, Georgia, who for four years labored with us in the development of Masterbrand Distributors. He died in the middle of June, 1996, aged 38.